Breeding Aquarium Fishes

Photo by Ruda Zukal.

by Dr. Herbert R. Axelrod

Distributed in the U.S.A. by T.F.H. Publications, Inc., P.O. Box 33, Jersey City, N.J. 07303; in England by T.F.H. (Gt. Britain) Ltd., 13 Nutley Lane, Reigate, Surrey; in Canada by Clarke, Irwin & Company, Clarwin House, 791 St. Clair Avenue West, Toronto 10, Ontario; in Southeast Asia by Y. W. Ong, 9 Lorong 36 Geylang, Singapore 14; in Australia and the south Pacific by Pet Imports Pty. Ltd., 38-40 Chard Road, Brookvale 2100, N.S.W., Australia.
The U.S.A. book trade distributors are Crown Publishers, Inc., 419 Park Avenue South, New York, N.Y. 10016.

Published by T.F.H. Publications, Inc. Ltd. The British Crown Colony of Hong Kong.

Dedicated to the two best aquarium photographers in the whole world, Hans Joachim Richter and Ruda Zukal. Without their help, this book would never have been.

TABLE OF CONTENTS

This book is a series of "chapters' dealing with the breeding habits of tropical aquarium fishes. It is the second volume in a series to be produced from time to time as enough material is collected to make a proper pictorial presentation of each subject. There is no index to this series since the chapters are inclusive of all the material pertaining to the fish under discussion. For a review of elementary breeding details, see the first sections in Book I.

INTRODUCTION

It is six years since I wrote Book I of this series. I didn't know at that time that there would be such a good reception to a book detailing the spawning activities of aquarium fishes, but I was deeply gratified that almost 100,000 copies of the first volume were sold in five years. Interestingly enough, a large number of copies were sold in Japan.

This second book was much easier to write than the first. During the period between these two books, my dear friend Hans Joachim Richter developed into a first-class photographer. He was already one of the world's most skillful fish breeders, and by matching his talents with my needs he took some very impressive spawning photographs. Without Jochen (my pet name for Hans Joachim), this book would have been much less informative.

Even as this book goes to press I am working on new ideas for the third book. It will, hopefully, contain information on breeding marine fishes, for there is a great need to know how to breed many of the food fishes both in fresh water and marine water. There is a great deal of activity, for instance, in breeding salmon, trout, and other important food fishes in *both* fresh water and brackish water.

This second book assumes that you have read the first book. Information about fishes' diets, spawning activities and other basic subjects are all discussed rather fully in Book I, so please refer to it before you tackle this volume unless you have some previous experience breeding the egglayers.

While many livebearing fishes, especially some of the exotic guppies, present challenging problems, the raising of these fancy varieties is more a problem of aquarium management than technique. Guppies will breed under almost any conditions that will keep them alive; this is not true of most of the egglaying fishes.

I sincerely hope that you find the information contained within these pages enables you to spawn a few fishes which you never thought possible before.

Herbert R. Axelrod

Hong Kong
September, 1971

A pair of *Pelmatochromis ansorgii* inspecting a possible spawning site. The female indicates her acceptance of the site by "dry running" the area. No eggs are laid at this time. Photo by Ruda Zukal.

The Five-Spot African Cichlid

Pelmatochromis ansorgii

The five-spot African cichlid, *Pelmatochromis ansorgii*, has been known to science since 1813 when Boulenger catalogued it. Live specimens were probably imported to Germany in the early 1900's, since this fish is quite common along the west African coast from Liberia to the Congo. The author caught several specimens in almost pure salt water along with *Monodactylus sebae* near Douala in the Cameroons. The largest specimen I have ever seen is slightly over 4 inches, but I never saw any this large in their natural range.

These three photos (see facing page) show the beginning of the egg-laying process. After several false spawning runs, the female finally lays eight eggs (photo above). The male is always attentive to the female and the selection of the spawning site may be made by the two fish together. Photos by Ruda Zukal.

The rather elongate body, large mouth and fleshy lips give this cichlid the appearance of a pugnacious fish, but just the converse is true. Except during breeding time, the fish is peaceful, subdued and shy. It might even be nocturnal, as its large eye could capture enough moonlight for it to graze at night. Certainly in the aquarium it hides at the slightest provocation and probably has lost most of its popularity because of this. It prefers dimly lit locations.

Since the female is responsible for the design of the nest, these three photographs (see facing page), show the stages in the design. The basic circle is always maintained and, once the nest has a circular shape, the female begins laying in circles, with her body twisting as she spawns. The eggs are very sticky and adhere to the slate as soon as they touch it. The opposite end of the egg becomes clouded and forms a polar cap on the elongated egg. The difference in heat conductivity between the water and the spawning site is not the cause of the polarization of the egg at the end opposite the point of attachment. Photos by Ruda Zukal.

As soon as the female deposits her eggs, about ten at a time, she leaves the spawning site, and the male immediately enters the area to fertilize the eggs (photos on facing page). The male, in the photo above, watches the egg-laying process carefully, and as soon as the female is finished depositing a row of eggs, he rushes in to add his sperm to the unfertilized eggs. Photos by Ruda Zukal.

I keep my fish in slightly salty water. Usually I add a gallon of sea water to every five gallons of aquarium water, but the same effect is achieved by putting in a few tablespoonfuls of sea salt (Kosher salt will do) for every 5 gallons. In order for the fish to be comfortable and acclimated, it is absolutely necessary that their aquarium be furnished with several inverted flowerpots, or, better yet, with caves made of flat stones. Unquestionably the fish will select one of these sites in which to spawn, if they were properly fed and brought into prime condition. The water temperature should always be above 70° F., and a 5° rise in temperature will usually start the spawning procedure if all else is in readiness.

As the male completes his fertilization of the eggs, and the nest gets larger and larger, the male may become distracted and become disturbed with the female laying more eggs. These three photos (see facing page) show the male fertilizing the nest, after which he attacked the female as she was adding a few more eggs to the already sizable spawn. Photos by Ruda Zukal.

Conditioning the breeders is very important. Pairs can be isolated in a 10 gallon aquarium with a gravel bottom and one or two rock caves as illustrated so well in the photographs. The fish do not, as a general rule, disturb the plants, so you can have the aquarium planted if you wish. I recommend isolation because the fish will almost always spawn, and it is a great pleasure to watch the mother swim about, herding and caring for the young. If other fishes are present they usually pick off the straggling babies, infuriating the breeders and causing them to eat their own offspring at times.

Above, the male fertilizes the entire nest, not just the eggs which were immediately previously deposited by the female. This seems to annoy the female, photo below, and she begins spawning again. Notice that her ovipositor touches the slate quite a distance from the eggs but she doesn't deposit any eggs until she senses they are adjacent to the nest. Photos by Ruda Zukal.

Above, the male sometimes begins to fertilize the eggs while the female is depositing them. This is usually a sign that he will soon lose interest in the nest; the female, photo below, seems to notice this also, and she watches more and more closely as spawning continues until finally, she lays her last eggs and chases the male away. Note the typical bright scales over her genital pore. Photos by Ruda Zukal.

To bring the five-spot African cichlid into spawning condition is merely a matter of proper feeding and relatively simple aquarium management. Feedings of live and freeze dried *Tubifex* are essential. The fish must have some vegetable matter in its diet, so feeding *Tubifex* worms with *Chlorella* algae (freeze dried form is now available) or Gordon's Formula which contains liver and spinach, is highly recommended. It only takes a few weeks before the fish become acclimated to their spawning aquarium and the female begins to fill up. As the female gets fatter, the male begins to take on his breeding colors, red-tinted body scales, and the usual brilliant, reflective blue shine to the ends of his dorsal, caudal and anal fins. Immediately before spawning, the male darkens considerably and the "five spots" become very evident.

The contrast in breeding coloration is quite obvious and sex differences become accentuated. Normally the male has much longer and more pointed fins and he shows his five spots more frequently than the female. The female shows, on the other hand, about five scales near the genital pore which become very shiny as she matures and ripens. At times she shows these brilliant specks on other parts of her lower abdomen, but only *during* the spawning process, not after.

Spawning takes place after the usual cichlid flirting, perhaps locking of jaws, and a few digging of holes in the gravel for the future storage of newly hatched fry. The pair usually select the most secluded place in the aquarium to spawn. This can be the top of the cave, the inside top of a flowerpot, or the corner of the aquarium if it is hidden and covered by plants. The female seems to be the one who selects the spawning site, and while they mouth each other preparatory to spawning, the female searches for a site upon which to deposit her eggs. As soon as she is ready to spawn, her ovipositor begins to appear from her anal pore. At this

Spawning has finally been completed and about 400 eggs were laid during the sequence in which these excellent Zukal photos were made. The female has now taken complete charge of the nest, which she guards quite vigorously against any other fish which tries to enter the cave . . . even the male that fathered the eggs! As the female guards the nest, she moves her fins vigorously, forcing water to flow through the cave, over the spawning site, aerating the developing eggs very satisfactorily. The eggs can be removed at this stage for artificial hatching, but they must be subjected to vigorous aeration if they are to hatch. Photo by Ruda Zukal.

time she makes a few "dry runs" in the area she has selected for spawning. If the male joins her at the spawning site, she will begin to lay her eggs in rows which crisscross each other, gradually forming a circle of about 2 inches in diameter. Sometimes as many as 800 eggs are laid. About 400 were laid during the spawning illustrated here.

The eggs are typical of most cichlids that lay hanging eggs. They are oval in shape, much like a chicken's egg, but much smaller, of course. They are cloudy when first laid, with a slightly yellow cast. Within a few moments of being laid they seem to swell and development starts at the pole of the egg farthest from the end of the egg which is attached at the spawning site.

Spawning lasts several hours and the male quickly loses interest in the eggs. Many breeders recommend removing the male immediately after spawning; I have had bad experiences where the male attacked the female while she was attending the eggs, but I enjoy watching the pair with the young. Most of the time they are eaten unless the male is removed.

The eggs hatch in two or three days depending upon the water temperature and the female tends to the eggs in a most peculiar way. Not only does she fan the eggs with her fins in the usual cichlid manner, but she sprays them with water from her mouth. You can actually perceive her taking mouthfuls of water and spitting it on the eggs. So powerful is the force of this expectoration that the eggs wave back and forth reacting to the strong force of the current generated by the flow from the female's mouth. Periodically, the female mouths the eggs and the unfertilized eggs assumedly burst from the rough treatment given them by the scouring.

The young are slow growing. They take newly hatched brine shrimp as soon as they are free swimming and have absorbed their yolk sacs.

A pair of *Corydoras funelli*. The female is larger than the male in length and girth. Prior to spawning, she is obviously ripe and full of eggs. Photo by Ruda Zukal.

Salt-and-Pepper Catfish

Corydoras funelli

The salt-and-pepper catfish has been known by many names. It is incorrectly recorded in books and magazines as *Corydoras schultzei*, but we will have to await the final word from such *Corydoras* experts as Dr. Stanley Weitzman before we can definitely commit ourselves to the correctness of the name.

All *Corydoras* are found in South America, from one tip (Trinidad) to the other (Argentina). Some have very restricted ranges and are found only in one small pool, while others are found all over considerably wide areas.

A bottom view of the spawning pair. Note the fullness of the female. Note that her ventral fins are almost fused when compared to those of the male. Photo by Ruda Zukal.

Some are very plentiful; in one area near Manacapuru, Amazon River, Brazil, I found a pond a few feet deep containing more than one million *Corydoras* per acre. Yet in the Rio Araguaia, I found a new species which was represented by only a single specimen.

I had always thought that all the *Corydoras* spawned alike. I have spawned some twenty-odd species and I still have not reached any definite conclusions. Probably all *Corydoras* can spawn alike, but not every species or every pair of individuals spawns the same way each time.

There is no question that considerable doubt exists about how the *Corydoras* species fertilize their eggs, so my report here about the spawning of *Corydoras funelli* will be based upon my own limited experience with this species, as well as the documented spawning photos taken by Rudi Zukal in Brno, Czechoslovakia.

Sexing the salt-and-pepper catfish is simple. The male is much smaller than the female and has a more pointed dorsal fin. There may be differences in other fins as well. When viewing from the top or bottom, the broadness and size of the female is obviously distinct from that of the male.

Two males are courting a female. One of the surest signs that spawning will shortly commence is the repetitious behavior of the male in placing himself in front of the female with her mouth close to his vent. Photo by Ruda Zukal.

Success by both Zukal and myself came when several males with twice as many females were used in a fairly well planted large aquarium. The fish must be fed heavily on live foods, especially *Tubifex* worms, which they seem to become addicted to. After a few days of heavy feeding, spawning begins.

The spawning activity starts with the fish, which previously have ignored each other, beginning to swim about each other in mid-water. Normally all *Corydoras* stay on the bottom most of the time, occasionally rising quickly to the surface for a bubble of air. When they remain in mid-water they may be sick or getting ready to spawn.

Immediately prior to spawning, the first sex-play act is the male mouthing the female all over her body. If she doesn't attempt to escape from the male's attentions, she will usually spawn. Photo by Ruda Zukal.

After having been mouthed by the male, the female directs her attention to the anal pore of the male where she may take sperm into her mouth. This action is hypothetical at the moment and no one has shown that this species actually does spawn with the female taking sperm into her mouth to fertilize her own eggs. Photo by Ruda Zukal.

A close look at the female might well intimate her readiness to spawn, and soon the pair drop to the bottom of the tank. Soon the male begins to mouth the female all over her body. As soon as he works his way up to her head, he will stop in front of her and place his vent very near to her mouth. Usually this action brings another male to the scene, but the first male is usually the one to successfully interest the female in going further. The female accepts the male by sucking on his ventral fins very near to his vent. This action has led me (and others) to suggest that she is taking a mouthful of sperm. Once this suction affects the male, he bends his body in an "S" quiver and assumedly releases his sperm. Sometimes at the same time the female releases from one to five eggs directly into her ventral pouch. This pouch is formed by the sticking together of her ventral fins during

As soon as the female's mouth touches the male's anal pore, he may tense and **"S"**-curve his body (photo below). The attention the female pays to the male's anal pore may be to collect sperm in her mouth. Photo by Ruda Zukal.

As soon as the female has attached herself to the male (above) and the male has done whatever he has to do in that position, he may swim away, clasping the female's barbels under his strong, serrated pectoral fin, as is so clearly shown in the remarkable photo below. Photos by Ruda Zukal.

As she spawns, the female lays her eggs into her own pelvic fins which have formed an egg pouch. The eggs are clearly visible through the pouch and she swims past three eggs previously laid on the glass. Zukal photo.

the spawning process. When not spawning, the fins are kept separate. Not only does this stickiness help form the ventral pouch, but it also helps to keep the eggs from falling out. It is quite possible that the eggs have been fertilized in this pouch by sperm released by the male when he "S"-curved and ejaculated. It is also possible that should there not have been any eggs in the female's pouch when the male ejaculated, the stickiness of the pouch picked up sperm which fertilized the subsequently released eggs. Should the female not have released her eggs after sucking near the male's vent, then she will release them immediately after she leaves the male.

For she immediately searches for a site upon which to deposit the eggs. Every spawning effort results in one to five eggs, each group of which is deposited at a different place. As soon as the female selects the spawning site, she gives it a thorough mouthing, cleaning it perhaps. Some authors claim that she places the sperm here as well, to fertilize those eggs which weren't already fertilized. As soon as she has cleaned the spot with her mouth, she presses her ventral pouch against the spot and the eggs adhere. The

Approaching the glass, and about to deposit a few sticky eggs against it, the female's egg pouch, formed by the fusion of her pelvic fins, becomes very obviously a carrying device under the female's control. No other fish has the ability to use its pelvic fins for carrying. Photo by Ruda Zukal.

As she approaches the glass and presses against it, she begins to relax her pelvic fins so the eggs can be pressed against the spawning site to which they will adhere. Photo by Ruda Zukal.

eggs are very sticky and require a razor blade to remove them. They are also very sticky while they are in the pouch of the female as they quickly pick up any floating debris or sand which might get mixed in with them. Eggs which have been "sanded" usually do not adhere to the glass or other attachment spot, but fall to the bottom. They hatch anyway.

Spawning continues for two or three months, with the fish laying eggs every two or three days (usually from February to April, which corresponds to the rainy season along the Brazilian Amazon). Each female can produce 100-200 eggs.

As her pelvic fins touch the glass, they spread apart and the eggs are attached to the glass. The spawning site in an aquarium is not always glass. It is often anything in the aquarium, from plants to heater tubes. Photo by Ruda Zukal.

The eggs hatch in about five days, and the fry absorb their large yolk sacs on the eighth day; they then have to be fed newly hatched brine shrimp and egg yolk infusion.

Since the eggs are laid all over the aquarium, the breeders should be removed after the fourth day and separated for a week before being allowed to spawn again. The parents usually eat the fry once they have hatched.

The young are ready to spawn the following February if they are well fed.

There are times when the male accompanies the female, on her search for a spawning site. Notice that the female has eggs in her pelvic pouch. In this series of photos, what *may* be illustrated is the female carrying unfertilized eggs. The male, accompanying her, selects a spawning site, and puts a sperm packet from his mouth against the site (see photos on facing page), after which the female deposits her eggs amidst the sperm. Photos by Ruda Zukal.

A pair of *Corydoras funelli* (above), female the larger and more plump of the two. Below, a female carrying eggs in her egg pouch formed by her pelvic fins. Photos by Ruda Zukal.

The new gold gourami male, a color variety of *Trichogaster trichopterus*, prepares a bubblenest. Photo by Hans Joachim Richter.

The Gold Gourami

Trichogaster trichopterus, golden variety

In 1970 East Germany had a very warm summer and several adventurous aquarists put some of their Cosby gouramis outside in sunken barrels, bathtubs and 55-gallon drums, and allowed them to spawn freely. The ordinary Cosby gourami is a natural for this kind of treatment since they are fairly hardy when kept above 70° and they have such huge spawns that breeding them in an aquarium is almost impossible since they could easily produce one thousand youngsters. Without anyone knowing why, the Communist market became glutted with small Cosby gouramis and the East Germans had a field day . . . at last some cheap fish!

As the fish grew up a startling development took place. *The pigment disappeared and the fish became golden.* This same phenomenon is to be observed in the golden angelfish, *Pterophyllum scalare.* Also, similar to the golden angelfish, as soon as breeders got the fish into their hands, they used those which turned golden the soonest for breeders until finally, by late 1971, golden-colored Cosby gouramis were available at low cost and when fairly young they show the gold.

The accompanying color photographs by Hans Joachim Richter clearly show the beauty and individuality of markings of this new mutant variety (which does not exist in this color format in the wild).

Breeding the golden variety is almost identical to breeding the normal Cosby variety, but allow me to report about the original spawning from which the accompanying photographs were made. According to Richter he used an aquarium which was 20 inches long and had a capacity of 10 gallons. It was very heavily planted so the female could find plenty of room to hide should the male become too aggressive. The

The "three spot blue" gourami which has almost no body markings except the very evident spots on the side. The "three spot" got its name from the uniform spacing of the eye and the two body spots which were "supposed to confuse a predatory fish." Photo by Günter Senfft.

temperature was raised to 77° or more and the fish had been fed a variety of live foods. According to Richter the water quality isn't very significant as regards hardness, pH or age, though it is to be recommended that the water lie between 6.0 and 8.0 in pH and not be too hard. Freshwater stimulates the fish to spawn, especially rainwater.

If a pair are suitably conditioned, and the female is plump as she fills with roe, the pair can be introduced to the spawning tank at any time. With a minimum of courtship, the male begins to build a huge bubblenest, usually under a floating leaf if it is available. The female just watches the male during this activity and she doesn't participate at all. As a matter of fact, should she come near the nest during the construction stage, the male will violently chase her away, *as though she were an enemy*.

As soon as the nest is built, a process which may take from a few hours to a few days, the male poses under the nest waiting for the female to come to him. She usually does come

The female gold gourami stimulates the male by probing his body, starting about the caudal base of the anal fin and working up to the base of the ventral fins. Photo by Hans Joachim Richter.

The male indicates his willingness to spawn by "inviting" the female under his nest. The curved position of their bodies is a natural consequence of their circling each other preparatory to embracing. Note the lack of marking in the female. Photo by Hans Joachim Richter.

(Above) Careful inbreeding by the Germans resulted in a strain of very dark blue, slightly mottled *Trichogaster trichopterus*. This male is in spawning color intensification. Photo by Gerhard Budich.

(Above facing page) The Czechs developed a variety of marbled *Trichogaster trichopterus* as illustrated above in a photo by Milan Chvojka. (Below facing page) The earliest Cosby gouramis, merely a color variety of *Trichogaster trichopterus*, were developed by a gentleman named Cosby in the United States. These fish do not appear as wild specimens. Photo by Dr. Herbert R. Axelrod.

As the pair enact their spawning embrace there might be several false starts. When eggs are not produced, the pair seem to have less intense coloration (see facing page). As soon as the eggs begin to appear, the color red intensifies in both male and female. Photos by Hans Joachim Richter.

to the male, though often the male searches her out. As she approaches the male, she mouths him in the area around his genital pore. Often she goes wide of the mark and may nip him at the base of his caudal fin. Once she excites the male with this action, the pair circle each other in a very tight formation, fins erect, until they settle into the typical anabantoid embrace which might be likened to a handshake, with each squeezing the other. As the embrace continues for 5-10 seconds, the male releases his sperm as evidenced by the cloud which appears near his vent. The eggs are then immediately released and they float through the cloud of sperm into the nest.

Trichogaster trichopterus, in all color varieties, are easily spawned together, regardless of color variety. This is brother and sister (male above), illustrating the variation which is normal in such color crossings. Photo by Gerhard Budich.

A top view of a bubblenest of *Trichogaster* showing the thousands of small black specks which are the babies. The *Trichogaster trichopterus* varieties are probably the easiest to spawn and most prolific of all the gouramis. Photo by Ruda Zukal.

Often the embrace is so *violent* . . . *amorous* might be a better word . . . that the nest becomes disturbed, or, as is more likely to happen, the eggs are not released into the nest but simply float up to the surface of the water. Neither case is very significant. The eggs can easily hatch without being a part of the nest and without having the devoted care of the father.

Under usual circumstances the male repairs the nest and guards the young until they are free-swimming. While the young hatch in 24 hours at about 80°, they take about three days to become free-swimming. This usually is determined by the absorption of the yolk sac. Once the sac is absorbed, the young swim freely.

During the pre-spawning play, should the male not build his nest, or should the female not care to spawn, there is a strong possibility of savage fighting.

Once the male entices the female under his nest of bubbles, the pair embrace (facing page) and, with the male doubling his body around the female, out fly the eggs, right into the nest. As the eggs are laid, the male releases a cloud of sperm. Photo by Hans Joachim Richter.

Commercially, I have spawned five pair at a time, always with an excess of females, say 5 males and 7 females, in a large 20 gallon (30 inches long) aquarium. The top is completely covered with floating water hyacinth. The fish all spawn at once, with females using different males at times. After spawning, I remove all but two males and as soon as the fry are free-swimming I remove those males as well. The fry grow quickly if they are raised outdoors with lots of food in a large, dirt-bottomed pool. They grow very slowly in an aquarium where they must be fed egg yolk and infusoria, followed by freshly hatched brine shrimp.

Mating a male Betta with a female *Macropodus cupanus dayi*

There is a great amount of confusion concerning the breeding of anabantoid fishes and much of this misinformation stems from the Innes book (*Exotic Aquarium Fishes* by William T. Innes) which, though hopelessly outdated now, was THE first really great book written about aquarium fishes.

In the Innes book we find the misleading information that *Macropodus cupanus dayi* spawns like other anabantoids, and, that anabantoids do not actually require atmospheric

Macropodus cupanus dayi males have longer fins than do the females. The color varies with fright, hunger, background and health. All the four fish illustrated here can be as clearly marked as the lower fish (a male). Compare this marking with the wild type *Betta* female on the facing page. Photo by Günter Senfft.

A wild type Siamese fightingfish female is marked almost identically with wild *Macropodus* (see facing page). Photo by G. J. M. Timmerman.

oxygen and if kept in a sealed bottle filled with water and no air bubble, they will live. *Both of these are untrue statements.*

Anabantoids require atmospheric air or they drown. I have lost thousands of paradise fish, *Macropodus opercularis*, and dwarf gouramis by trapping them and other anabantoids in submerged plastic traps in pools in Florida, only to have them suffocate when I left the traps in the water overnight! Further, *Macropodus cupanus dayi* breeds *unlike* most common aquarium anabantoids in that they may actually construct a nest under a rock or in a cave.

But what may be the greatest error of all is the belief that if two fishes interbreed either in the aquarium or in the wild they must be the same species. This is especially true of

(Above) This is the male Siamese fighting fish, *Betta splendens*, which built a bubblenest in the presence of a female *Macropodus cupanus dayi*. Photo by Hans Joachim Richter.

(Facing page) The male *Betta* reacts to the female *Macropodus* in the same manner as he would towards a female of his own species. The same is true of the female *Macropodus*. She doesn't seem to identify the male *Betta* as a fish belonging to a different genus. Photo by Hans Joachim Richter.

Macropodus cupanus cupanus preparing to spawn. The lighter fish is the male and he is nudging a plump female. Photo by Ruda Zukal.

many *Symphysodon* (discus) breeders who think all the discus are the same species because they freely interbreed. Not only has Scheel proven this is not true for rivulins (see his excellent book *Rivulins of the Old World*), but no less an authority than Carl L. Hubbs in his 1955 article "Hybridization between fish species in nature" (*Syst. Zool. 4(1) :1-20*) emphatically declares that valid species often hybridize readily under laboratory (aquarium) conditions or in the wild. Schultz and Miller, while discussing the speciation problem in mollies "Species of the *Poecilia sphenops* complex in Mexico," *Copeia, 1971, (2) :282-290*) concur with Hubbs and go on to generalize that "*What determines specific status is the extent of gene flow between natural populations. If this is inadequate to cause convergence in nature, the species remain separate, even though they form hybrid swarms in localized parts of their overlapping ranges.*"

Macropodus cupanus cupanus is very closely related to *Macropodus cupanus dayi* and, while the names indicate they are sub-species, some ichthyologists separate them into two different species, namely *Macropodus dayi* and *Macropodus cupanus*. There is very little real comparison between the two sub-species in terms of outside appearances, and it would be very interesting to cross this fish with the *Betta*, too.

The male *Betta* spreads his fins to entice the female *Macropodus* into a spawning embrace under his nest. Photo by Hans Joachim Richter.

The "odd couple" seem a bit clumsy in their spawning attempts. Photo by Hans Joachim Richter.

A wild female *Macropodus cupanus dayi*, except for her fins (compare the dorsal fins and shape of the tail), looks very much like the wild female *Betta* in the top photo on the facing page. Photo by G. J. M. Timmerman.

The probing camera and scientific curiosity of Hans Joachim Richter has focused attention on a peculiar cross between a Siamese fighting fish, *Betta splendens*, male and a female *Macropodus cupanus dayi*. In his description he says that in situations where a lone *dayi* female, without a male of her own species available, is maintained with a lone *Betta* male, without a female of his own available, breeding takes place. He describes the actions of the male as being typical, with the usual bubblenest being constructed. The female *dayi* whose pre-spawning activities are normally similar to those of bettas, attracts and embraces the male under the nest, and the sinking eggs are picked up by both male and female and placed into the nest. The two spawnings referred to by Richter indicate that the young never reached the

(Above)Wild Siamese fightingfish. Photo by G. J. M. Timmerman. (Below) Three male Siamese fightingfish, under stress, show the wild striped pattern which is so similar to the *Macropodus cupanus dayi* pattern. Photo by Robert E. Gossington.

Finally, after several false starts, the male *Betta splendens* and the female *Macropodus cupanus dayi* find the correct position. The female was extremely cooperative. Photo by Hans Joachim Richter.

The spawning embrace is finally consummated in the usual manner, directly under the bubblenest. Photo by Hans Joachim Richter.

The normal embrace of Siamese fightingfish as the eggs are dropping from the spawning pair. Photo by Dr. Herbert R. Axelrod.

The female fightingfish remains paralyzed after the embrace as the male gathers the eggs in his mouth preparatory to spitting them into the bubble-nest. Photo by Dr. Herbert R. Axelrod.

The heavier-than-water eggs slowly fall to the bottom of the tank as the pair spawn. The male (facing page) quickly dives to get the eggs before they get lost in the gravel at the bottom of the aquarium. Eggs which have fallen into the stones are sought and blown into the nest with the rest of the eggs. Photos by Hans Joachim Richter.

Siamese fightingfish males are very aggressive as illustrated by the two fighting males in this photograph. One advantage of a cross between the *Betta* and *Macropodus* might be in a more peaceful hybrid. Photo by G. J. M. Timmerman.

free-swimming stage, though they did hatch and develop into recognizable individuals. This might be similar to the "belly-sliders" which often result from rivulin hybridization and which is quite familiar to all killifish breeders.

From my own experience it would indicate that the fishes would, sooner or later, yield some viable offspring, but it would be very questionable whether the fry produced by the hybrids would be viable or not. A more interesting question for hobbyists might be the reasons for trying to cross a *Betta,* which is probably the most colorful and variable of all aquarium egglayers, with *Macropodus cupanus dayi* which is one of the least colorful of all anabantoids?

One of the answers would be that bettas are expensive because the males have to be raised in separate containers, requiring quite a bit of handwork in their daily feeding, weekly cleaning and individual shipping requirements. If the relative peacefulness of the *Macropodus* could be matched with the color of the *Betta*, the price of the hybrid would be considerably less than normal bettas now cost and hobbyists could enjoy more than one male *Betta* per tank. Can you imagine what an aquarium full of different colored male bettas would look like?

Further advantages of the hybrid might be longer fins in both males and females since *Macropodus* males and females have fins of similar shape and size.

The final and most interesting possibility might be the change in inheritance in the hybrid to where spotted,

Not all *Betta* are showy, flashy fish. This is the usual poor conditioned fightingfish. A hybrid might result in a stronger strain.

As the spawning commences, the nest gets larger and larger, higher and higher, as the male adds eggs and bubbles. The female *Macropodus* does not normally attend the nest in any way. Photo by Hans Joachim Richter.

blotched offspring might result rather than relatively uniform colored offspring usual with the crossing of normal bettas of different coloration. An example of this type of inheritance might be of breeding two dogs. Crossing a white poodle and black poodle might easily produce a parti-colored or "spot" poodle instead of a gray poodle which would be a mixture of the black and white colors of the parents.

More hobbyists . . . and scientists . . . should try to breed some of those fishes which have such similar spawning habits, and they should report their findings, like Richter did, in hobbyist magazines.

Once spawning is completed the male will viciously reject the female and might even kill her, but while the female still is swollen with eggs, she is the aggressor! Photo by Hans Joachim Richter.

Young pairs can spawn before the male attains his secondary sex characteristics of extended dorsal fin rays. This young pair spawned for the photographer Ruda Zukal.

The Longfin Barb

Capoeta arulius

Barbs are found throughout India, and this beauty is one of the most lively barbs to be found on continental Asia. I

A young pair of longfin barbs. The slightly more slender fish, above, is the male. When he matures his dorsal rays will become extended. Photo by Ruda Zukal.

have found them within 50 miles of Bombay, though the literature cites their range as northeast of Bombay and near Travancore and Canvery. Anyway, in the wild they are absolutely stunning, especially the males with their elongated dorsal rays and scarlet fins.

One of the advantages of this barb is its peacefulness. Kept in an aquarium as a sole member of its species, the fish hides and gets lost in the foliage; but put it in with 20 other barbs, any kind of barbs, and it becomes active and much more colorful. I have never known a longfin barb to aggravate other fishes the way the tetrazona barb harasses any fish with long fins (like gouramies or angelfish).

To bring the fish into the best of condition I would suggest that you set up two 20 gallon, thirty-inch aquariums. Keep the males in one aquarium and the females in the other, with a water temperature close to 80°. The males will color up first, and this coloration is almost always a green sheen on the

(Above) A mature pair of *Puntius arulius*. The male, upper fish, has extended filaments in his dorsal fin. Photo by Dr. Herbert R. Axelrod. (Below) A very young pair of *arulius*, female below. Photo by Ruda Zukal.

The pair indicate their willingness to spawn by swimming in small circles close to a suitable spawning site, like the bushy plants in the background. Photo by Ruda Zukal.

scales running along the sides of the fish. Soon the female also develops this greenish iridescence and she begins to swell with eggs. Don't wait too long when she is in this condition as she might well become eggbound and die.

Immediately place spawning grass in dense clumps all about the bottom of the tank. As you will have observed, these fish hug the bottom of the tank most of the time, and spawning time is no different.

Now remove half the females and place them in with the males, while at the same time removing half the males from the other tank and placing them in with the females. Depending upon which are more prepared for spawning, I have found that the aquarium in which the females were introduced spawns first; the aquarium into which the males were introduced takes longer to spawn since the males are more inhibited when they are in new circumstances.

Almost as soon as the pair of longfin barbs have suitable conditions, the males begin to chase the females. The chasing goes on for hours. Photos by Ruda Zukal.

As the female becomes more receptive, she slows down and allows the male to line up alongside. Then (below) she butts him near his vent as a sign of acceptance. Photos by Ruda Zukal.

It is possible that the female is actually worn down by the constant chasing of the male, for her mouth is gasping huge amounts of water during this process. Photo by Ruda Zukal.

The pair head for bushy plants to release their spawn. Photo by Ruda Zukal.

During spawning, the pair line up, with bodies parallel to each other, nose to nose. The male seems to be the "driver" and he pushes and directs the female into the thickets. Photo by Ruda Zukal.

The spawning embrace takes place so fast, that until the strobe camera "stopped" the action, no one ever recorded the fact that the male wraps his body about that of the female. Here is the photographic evidence. Photo by Ruda Zukal.

The three photographs on these facing pages show, for the first time, how the *arulius* male wraps his body about the female during the spawning process. Photos by Ruda Zukal.

Spawning is a wild chase all around the bottom of the tank until the male finally traps the female in the spawning grass and wraps his body around her in such a way that it reminds one of a gourami spawning! First the male lines himself up side-by-side with the female. Then, keeping the cheek-to-cheek position, the male twists the rear half of his body over the top of the female, in back of her dorsal fin, and out come the eggs. The accompanying photographs show much more detail of this spawning act. *Rasbora heteromorpha*, as well as other members of the Cyprinidae, also have this same spawning habit.

In soft water, with a neutral pH, you should not have any problem with breeders or their fry. Spawning takes an afternoon or morning, about four hours, and with a fully mature pair, almost 500 babies can be the result.

The eggs hatch in less than two days and the fry are free-swimming four days later. Infusoria and freshly-hatched brine shrimp are perfect food for the first week, after which they eat anything that is fine enough for them to swallow whole.

(Above) A male *Polycentrus schomburgki*, just beginning to show his coloration. While on the facing page, we see a pair of *schomburgki*, female the upper fish. Photos by Ruda Zukal.

Schomburgk's Leaf Fish

Polycentrus schomburgki

I have found almost all the new fishes I discovered in small streams, waist deep in most cases, with overhanging, densely vegetated banks. In nearly every stream I fished in northern South America I found these leaf fish hiding among the matted vegetation. I have never seen one swimming in open water and, from the observation of their habits in the aquarium, I assume they are nocturnal in habit.

The way I have broken them of this habit in the aquarium has been to merely leave the light on 24 hours a day, a method I use for all my fishes to induce them to spawn "out of season" should they be seasonal in their spawning cycle.

This leaf fish is not for the beginner. The only way they can successfully be reared and brought into breeding

(Above) The male as he has just matured and is interested in spawning. (Below) He inspects various spawning sites and seems to have decided upon the underside of an Amazon swordplant leaf. Photos by Ruda Zukal.

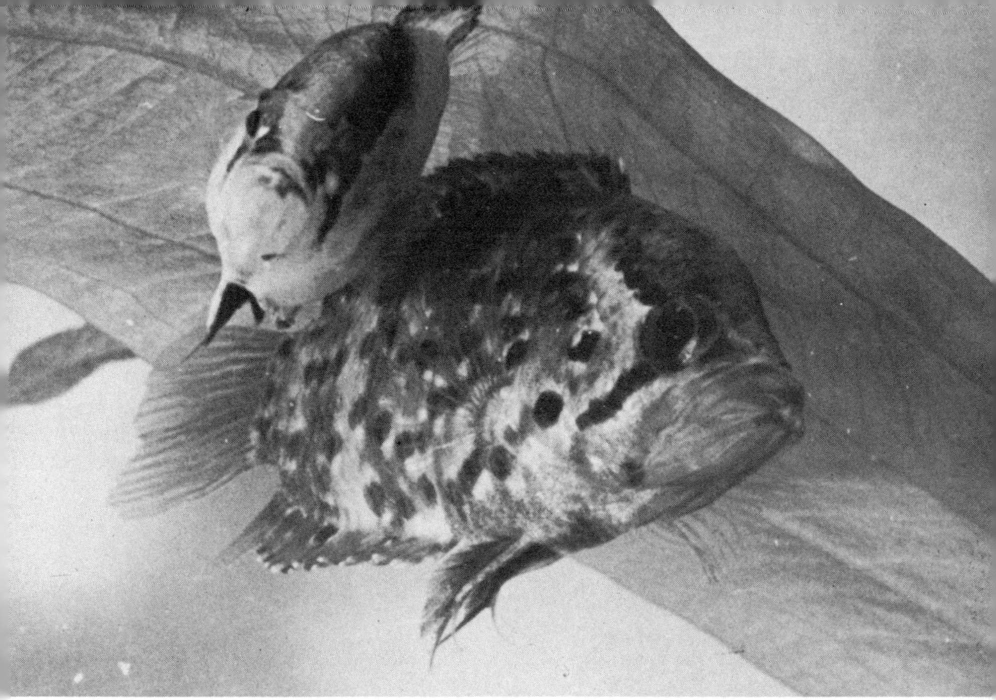

(Above) Having found a bulging, ripe female, the male shows her the spawning site of his choice. (Below) The female indicates her acceptance of the spawning site by "biting" at the leaf, seemingly an act of housekeeping. This excites the male and he gently nips her in the region of her genital pore. Photos by Ruda Zukal.

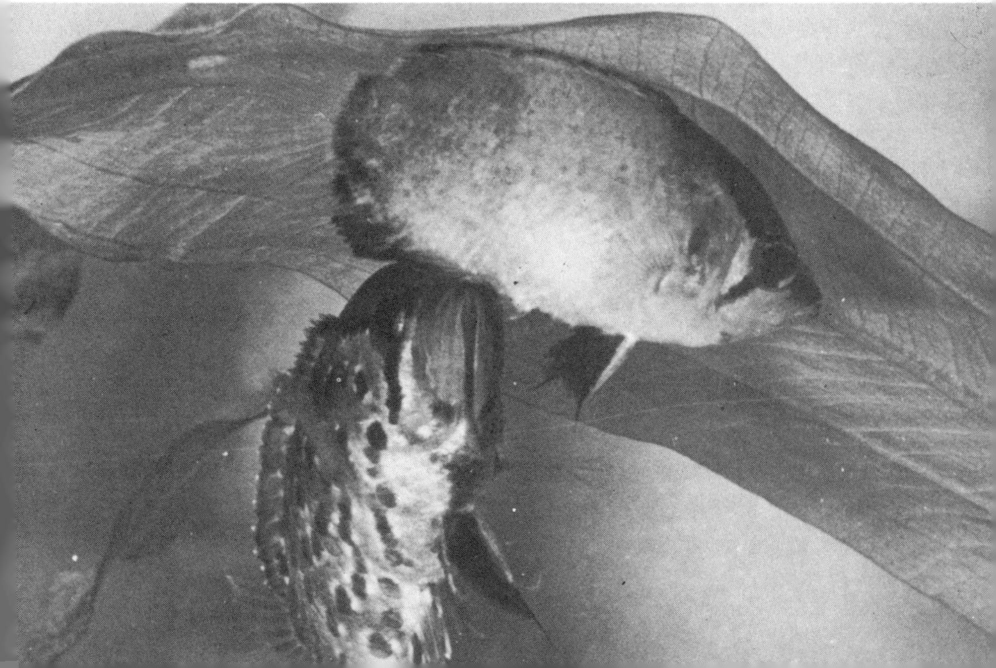

Very young leaf fish show the mottling characteristic of both sexes, but even young fish are dangerous to other fishes small enough to be swallowed whole. Photo by Dr. Stanislav Frank.

condition is with huge quantities of small, live fishes. An adult can eat its own weight of guppies in a few days. Their appetites are almost insatiable! Having met their conditions successfully, however, they spawn readily. The following recommendations have been utilized by the professionals.

A pair of leaf fish is maintained in a small aquarium (5 gallons is very large for them), in which there is very heavy, dense vegetation. The preferred spawning site is the leaf of sturdy Amazon swordplant, either living or plastic. The water should be as soft as possible, with a neutral pH. I have been very successful in spawning them in hard water, even water containing as much as a teaspoonful of salt per gallon. They do not seem to be very particular about the pH or softness of the water, but their fry seem to do better in soft, neutral to slightly alkaline water.

Sexing the fish is relatively simple. During their breeding cycle, the male is an intense dark color, almost black, while the female is almost white. The males are larger than the females. During their resting stages (non-spawning) they are also distinctive. The female is a creamy pink, while the male is a dead-leaf brown, with bold spots arranged leopard-like all over his body, dorsal and anal fins. The accompanying color photographs clearly show the sex differences during both stages.

To bring the fish to breeding condition, place the pair in the spawning tank along with a few dozen small guppies about a month old. Small male guppies are also welcome food for these hungry creatures. Heavy female guppies may be added and as they drop their living young, the leaf fish will gobble them up. I have had occasion, however, when the leaf fish also ate the female guppies, as their huge protractile mouths expand considerably. After a few weeks of feeding heavily with live foods, gradually raise the temperature of

As spawning time approaches, the male gets blacker and blacker while the female manifests her very obvious ovipositor, the tube through which her eggs will pass. Photo by Ruda Zukal.

(Above) The female is coaxed into position under the Amazon swordplant leaf as the pair attain startling color changes. (Below) She then turns, belly up, and begins to deposit her spawn on the underside of the leaf. Photos by Ruda Zukal.

(Above) The pair remain at the spawning site during the entire egg-laying period. (Below) The male guards the nest more and more intently, even while the female is still spawning. Should the female peck at the eggs with her mouth, she might be ferociously attacked by the male. Photos by Ruda Zukal.

the water to about 82°F. The female should develop an obvious nipple near her vent. This will be the beginning of the protrusion of her ovipositor (the egg-laying tube); the male will get darker, too.

Soon the pair will begin looking for a spawning site. This will almost always be the underside of a broad leaf or the bottom of a submerged branch. At times the parents-to-be will clean the area with their mouths, but usually they do little in the way of spawning site sanitation. A sure sign that spawning is imminent is that the pair will remain close together in the upper parts of the aquarium, under a leaf. Normally they are hidden and relatively far away from each other.

Finally the pair begin to spawn, and by this time the male is almost an intense onyx black, while the female has lost all of her color and is an alabaster yellow-pink. The female begins the spawning act after the usual belly-butting

The female continues laying eggs and, while it is normal for the male to fertilize the eggs after the female has left, this photo shows the characteristic tilt of his body while he releases the sperm which floats up to fertilize the eggs. The male has never been observed to fertilize the eggs in the upside-down position utilized by the female to deposit her spawn. Photo by Ruda Zukal.

This closeup shows the ovipositor of the female actually pressing against the leaf as she expels her egg. The darkened male is guarding the spawning site and fertilizing the eggs as the female lays them. Photo by Ruda Zukal.

through which many tropical aquarium fishes proceed. She turns belly up and lays a few eggs. The eggs are very adhesive and stick immediately to the spot on which they were laid. After laying these few eggs, the female returns to a "neutral corner" and allows the male to fertilize the eggs. He does this in a very interesting manner: he takes a position almost directly under the eggs, turns his body at a very slight

(Above) This bottom view clearly shows the ovipositor's position near the bottom centerline of the female. The male stays very dark in color while spawning is in progress. (Below) As soon as the female has just about deposited all her spawn, the male lightens in color and chases the female away from the nest. Photos by Ruda Zukal.

As the eggs hatch, the young stick to the leaf, but their vigorous wriggling soon detaches them and they fall to the bottom of the aquarium where they remain until they have absorbed their yolk sacs and become free-swimming, searching for food. Photo by Ruda Zukal.

angle, and releases a cloud of sperm with a very obvious shuddering tremble, which floats up immediately and fertilizes the eggs. In short order, the female returns, lays more eggs, and the whole process starts again. This spawning keeps up for a whole morning or afternoon, until 400-500 eggs are laid. Oftentimes the male will release his sperm while the female is laying her eggs, but I have never seen him assume the belly-up position of the female. The spawning site with all its eggs, is not a neat, uniform sort of thing. It looks like it was made by leaf fish which are themselves not neat looking things!

After two days, when the eggs have hatched, I discovered that the male didn't play the role of the protective father, so he was removed. The third day after being laid, the hatched eggs wriggled vigorously and the hatchlings fell to the bottom of the tank. The remaining guppies will eat the babies immediately after having removed the parents, so be sure to remove the uneaten guppies as soon as the ovipositor protrudes from the female.

A week after the eggs were laid, the fry are free-swimming and hunting for food. The fry are very large and eat quantities of freshly hatched brine shrimp.

A mature male croaking gourami, *Trichopsis vittatus*. This is the usual coloration of the non-sexually-excited fish. Photo by Ruda Zukal.

The Croaking Gourami

Trichopsis vittatus

One of my many weaknesses has been for blue eyes (both in blondes and in fishes!) and wouldn't the croaking gourami be the exact same thing as a pretty blonde? *That's because it makes so much noise along with its pretty eyes!* This fish, to be serious, is one of the few tropical aquarium fishes which makes a lot of noise. The amount, intensity, duration and quality of the noise it makes varies tremendously with the fish and their aquarium conditions, for certain of my associates have *never* heard them croak!

Aside from their pretty eyes and noisemaking, this fish has other things to speak for it. First, it is most *unpopular*.

(Above) The mature female *Trichopsis vittatus*, swollen with eggs and in breeding color. (Below) The male, now sexually stimulated, begins to take on more color. Note the elongated rays in his unpaired fins. Photos by Ruda Zukal.

(Above) The unexcited pair of croaking gouramis feeding from the bottom as they search for *Tubifex* worms, a favorite food. (Below) Males sometimes flare up at each other, but they are not as active and aggressive as the related Siamese fightingfish, *Betta splendens*. Photos by Ruda Zukal.

(Above) Sexually stimulated males become more intensely colored and much more active. They spread their fins to every fish approaching them whether it be male or female. (Below) A male not ready for spawning has no intense coloration and he rarely swims with open fins. Photos by Ruda Zukal.

The male croaking gourami as he dances in front of the female of his choice. Rapid color changes are characteristic of the entire spawning process. Photo by Ruda Zukal.

The reason for this unpopularity is that it lacks the flamboyance, color and pugnaciousness of its cousin, the Siamese fighting fish. But once this ordinary looking fish gets itself into breeding condition, it at least has a chance to catch your eye. The relatively long fins, the very interesting breeding habits, and the fact that the female of the species will breed with just about any other same size anabantoid that makes a bubblenest, makes this a great fish for the more advanced aquarist.

Getting down to the serious business of making a bubblenest, the male croaking gourami has selected the underside of a floating leaf. Croaking gouramis, unlike many other gouramis, build their bubblenest under the water and not floating. Photos by Ruda Zukal.

The male croaking gourami, now darkened, attracts the female to the spawning site which she obviously approves. Photos by Ruda Zukal.

The male immediately begins building the nest and then beckons the female to see the construction. Photos by Ruda Zukal.

In the photo above, and on the facing page, is a rapid sequence showing the actual embrace and spawning of the croaking gourami. This embrace is characteristic of most anabantids. Photos by Ruda Zukal.

The pair are usually easy to sex since the male, once fully mature, will grow extended fin rays from his anal, caudal and dorsal fins. The female's fins are more normal. The female, when ripe with eggs, is much thicker than the male, especially when viewed from above. The pair can be brought to breeding condition by keeping them separate in a pint glass or plastic container floating in a thermostatically controlled heated aquarium, if you like. Feed the pair as much live food and freeze-dried food as possible. Flake foods do not put on body, for some reason. Baby guppies, live tubifex worms, brine shrimp (freeze-dried or live) and daphnia, are ideal foods.

Often the initial embrace fails to produce any eggs, as was the case here, but the male continues to build his nest, unaware of his lack of success. The female (below) initiates further spawning by butting the male near his underbelly region. Photos by Ruda Zukal.

The pair attempt to produce eggs again, right under the nest this time, even though the eggs will sink and not float into the nest, as with *Trichogaster trichopterus*, for example. Photos by Ruda Zukal.

The male wraps his body about the female and the pair roll over. As the eggs appear, the female falls into a trance and doesn't move. Photo by Ruda Zukal.

Once the female fattens up and the male begins to get brighter colors, they may be transferred to a small aquarium which is planted with a solitary large-leaved plant like an Amazon swordplant (live or plastic, doesn't matter), or a *Cryptocoryne* in a small flowerpot. The aquarium can contain freshly conditioned water and the temperature should be the same as that from which the fish came. Slowly raise the temperature in the aquarium (I use a 2 gallon aquarium very successfully), until the reading is either 85° or 10° higher than it was previously, whichever is lower. Within a few hours the pair should spawn . . . it's that easy.

Spawning is not exactly typical. Instead of building a bubblenest at the surface of the water as Siamese fighting fish, this fish builds a bubblenest under the water, usually trapping his bubbles in a hollow under a submerged leaf, such as is illustrated in the accompanying photographs.

Once the nest is built, the female approaches the male in typical gourami style, butting and biting him gently around his anal fin base, until he bends his body into an accommodation for her. Then the pair dance about each other with spread fins until they jockey into the typical handshake position wherein both fish almost bend in half wrapped about each other. As they squeeze each other, they roll about until about a dozen eggs are squeezed out of the female through a very fine cloud of sperm squeezed out of the male at the same time. The male quickly ends the embrace (handshake) as soon as he sees the eggs, but the female continues in her reverie and only "comes to" after the male has collected most of the eggs in his mouth and has

The male has been busy catching the slowly falling eggs in his mouth, preparatory to blowing them into the nest, while the female recovers from her "trance". Photo by Ruda Zukal.

blown them into the nest. Sometimes the eggs are scattered and the male will miss a few. Should the female see these eggs, she'll probably eat them.

The male as he catches four eggs (as clusters of two) right under his bubblenest where he just spawned with the female. Photo by Ruda Zukal.

At 85° the eggs hatch in about a day and the fry hang, like slivers of glass, from their nest. In another day they are to be found clinging to the glass, spread all over the tank, despite the effort of their father to keep them together in the nest. Removing the female after spawning is wise as the male might attack her whilst guarding the fry. Remove the male as soon as the fry are free-swimming, which is usually three days after hatching.

The eggs hatch in the submerged bubblenest and the young hang, head up, like little splinters until they are free swimming. Photo by Ruda Zukal.

The fry require either real, live infusoria, or the yolk of a hardboiled egg which has been squeezed through a nylon handkerchief. As soon as the fry take newly-hatched brine shrimp about a week later, they grow rapidly.

The croaking gourami is found in the wild all over the Indochina, Cambodia, Malaya, Indonesia area in shallow pools and streams. They are very common and can often be seen breaking the water for their gulp of atmospheric air. In an experiment I made with seven fish in Florida, I placed them into jars which had a net over the top. I sank the jars into an aquarium so all the air would escape from the jars. Within 24 hours all the fish had died, demonstrating that these fish *must* have atmospheric air to breathe or they drown.

The four photographs by Hans Joachim Richter, show the pair of comb-tails in all phases of their spawning activity: first, the pair find each other and engage in some playful biting. Then, below, they situate themselves under a floating leaf and embrace. On the facing page are photographs of the actual embrace and the release of the eggs by the female. The male has elongated unpaired fin rays.

The Comb-tail

Belontia signata

Sexing may be difficult for beginners as both fish might look alike. Photo by G. J. M. Timmerman.

Rodney Jonklaas knows more about the freshwater and marine fishes of his native Ceylon than anyone else in the world and the many times I've fished in Ceylon, Rodney's help has been readily available. So, as a tribute to Rodney and his unselfishness, I will generalize again and say that without Rodney there wouldn't be many Ceylonese fishes on the world aquarium market . . . and that means that there wouldn't be any comb-tails around either.

I had my first experience with comb-tails in 1952 when I brought back 5,000 on a ship from Hong Kong. The seven week trip resulted in a loss of more than 50% of all my 400,000 fishes, including *Rasbora heteromorpha,* but I didn't lose a single *Belontia.* As I got the fish into Staten Island harbor on September 17, 1952 (I'll never forget that day), it snowed! It hasn't snowed earlier than December 4th ever since!

I was very short of aquariums when I landed in New York with that large shipment and, knowing the comb-tails had been shipped by boat from Colombo, Ceylon to Hong Kong and from Hong Kong to New York without a casualty, I gambled further and put 200 five inch fish in a 30 inch long 20 gallon aquarium and hoped for the best. Except for a few that committed suicide (they jumped out of the tank), I didn't lose a fish! But something did happen that is worth mentioning.

As I walked past the tank one morning, a large *Astronotus* jumped out of the aquarium in which it was kept. I quickly lifted it off the floor and dumped it into the first tank at hand . . . and this tank happened to be the tank full of comb-tails.

The male comb-tail has longer unpaired fins which, in good specimens, are clearly visible. This fish has a crustacean parasite on his caudal peduncle, attached under a scale and about six scales long. Photo by Günter Sennfft.

Within 20 seconds the comb-tails had torn the six inch *Astronotus* to bits and within a further five minutes there was only a skeleton left! Obviously I wouldn't try to duplicate my feat with a more timid fish, but I'm certain they would do the same thing to a piranha.

Rodney and I collected some beautiful comb-tails in Ceylon and they were so red as to be unrecognizable from any I had ever before seen. This beautiful red color, however, quickly fades and, even when the fish is spawning, never seems to return. Perhaps this is because of their native water. I measured the hardness as being as soft as rainwater, with a pH of 6.7 and a temperature of 84°F. Though the sexes were difficult to determine on the small specimens, the larger fish about three inches long and longer, were fairly

A few bubbles are about all that the careless male *Belontia* bothered with as he built his bubblenest. The pair begin an embrace. Photo by Hans Joachim Richter.

The eggs fly from the female, as she becomes paralyzed in a belly-up position, under the nest. Photo by Hans Joachim Richter..

easy. The male was unquestionably thinner, especially after eating, than the fatter female. Of course once the female ripens with eggs, the plumpness is much more obvious.

Color is no sexual characteristic as far as I know, but the males get their color of excitation more rapidly than do the females. The color of excitation is an uneven barred pattern on the back above the lateral line with six or seven bars becoming fairly obvious, while below the lateral line the bars become chevron-shaped rows of dark scales. As the state of excitation advances, the juvenile ocellus (eye-spot) appears on the last rays of the dorsal fin base (see the color picture of the young).

If you only have a pair of comb-tails they must be treated like Siamese fighting fish and the pair must be kept separated or there might be trouble between these biting fish. I usually place the male in a large thirty-inch, twenty gallon aquarium by himself for a few days while I allow him to eat as many live guppies and freeze-dried tubifex worms as he wishes. Separated from him, but in the same tank, is a female. She gets the same food and the same treatment. The male's side containes a flowerpot with a plastic Amazon swordplant. The leaves drooped in such a way that they float slightly beneath the water's surface. In a day, as I raised the temperature from 75° to 85°, the male started to make a bubblenest under the floating plastic leaf. The nest wasn't a masterpiece and probably is being phased out of the evolution of the fish since the fish Rodney and I caught showed no evidence of inhabiting still waters where a bubblenest would stay together.

As soon as the male began building the nest, the female attempted to get through the tank divider I had separating them. (The tank divider was given to me by Penn Plax Company and is available, I am told, in every petshop). The advantage of this tank divider is that it can be removed easily without disturbing the delicate bubblenest, thus disturbing the breeders.

As the divider was removed, so was the resistance of the female and she immediately swam to the male's side. Both playfully bit each others' sides and attempted a few embraces, until they finally squeezed about 20 eggs out. The eggs floated slowly to the surface, during which time the male seems more concerned about getting the female out of the area than caring for the eggs, for he immediately attacks her, chasing her away, and then gathers the eggs in his mouth to blow them into his crude, two inch diameter nest under the floating plastic leaf. This goes on from high noon until about two hours before sunset. Perhaps 500 to 1,000 eggs are laid. Once the pair stop spawning, the male

The lower fish is the male and he begins his sex play with a biting attack against the female *Belontia*. Photo by G. J. M. Timmerman.

pays little if any further attention to the female, even allowing her to come very near the nest.

As their sexual coloration fades, the bite marks on both fish, but especially the female, becomes very obvious and I removed her and let her rest for a few days in an aquarium with some tetracycline and methylene blue added (500 mg. of tetracycline per five gallons and five drops of 5% methylene blue per gallon per day). I never lost a female by using this prophylactic treatment.

In the meantime, the male is left guarding the nest of pale, amber-colored eggs which seemed huge (they measured about $1\frac{1}{4}$ mm in diameter) and which had all hatched by the following evening. I allowed the temperature of the water to continue to rise and it was now over 90°F. Perhaps this hastened the hatching. In a few hours the male seemed to lose interest in the fry which were hanging from the glass sides of the aquarium, so he should be removed too. He can be

Young *Belontia* have an ocellus (eye spot) which disappears as the fish get older. Photo by Hans Joachim Richter.

removed anytime as he doesn't serve much useful purpose as his typical anabantoid "training" seems to be evolutionizing out. In another 72 hours the fry were free-swimming, had absorbed their yolk sacs and were searching for food. As soon as they eat freshly-hatched brine shrimp, their color becomes a dark brownish black, until at about three weeks of age they develop the typical eye spot on their dorsal base. As they grow, they should be thinned out and heavily fed. Sell them as quickly as you can because they start growing very fast and get very nasty unless they are kept with larger fish, especially cichlids.

The photography illustrating the details of the spawning of this *Pelvicachromis* species illustrates the main reasons for the popularity of dwarf cichlids. Not only do the fishes continually change color, as evidenced by the non-sexually stimulated male on the left compared to the sexually stimulated male on the right, but their actions in spawning and fry care are predictable and are the basis of most of fish behavioral science.

Photos in this series by Hans Joachim Richter.

Richter's Dwarf Cichlid

Pelvicachromis species

On the left is a non-sexually stimulated female, while on the right is the same female about to enter the cave of the male.

The nomenclature of this fish is very difficult to determine since specimens are not available from the original stock from the wild and I have my doubts that this is indeed a non-hybrid species.

The only information available on this fish comes from Hans Joachim Richter who lives in Leipzig, East Germany. Richter spawned the fish and wrote about them for me. He called them *Pelmatochromis klugei II*, but since that time the names of most of the *Pelmatochromis* have been changed to *Pelvicachromis*, and *P. klugei* has been determined as *P. taeniatus;* but this is definitely not *P. taeniatus* and without knowing the exact area from which this fish is found and without having specimens from the wild, it is impossible to determine the species and give it a valid scientific name.

I have proposed the name "Richter's dwarf cichlid" as this is what I have called it when discussing it with my colleagues, and I hope that whichever scientist actually does find specimens from the wild, he will officially name it *Pelvicachromis richteri,* to honor H. J. Richter. The following report from Richter clarifies the care and breeding of this philanderer:

In June, 1966 I was impatiently waiting for an announced shipment of fish from my friend Dr. Werny, of Saarbrücken, Germany. Besides several species of *Apistogramma* the shipment was supposed to include some specimens of *Pelmatochromis klugei II,* a fish I had never seen before. Of course I was very eager to find out what differences separate *P. klugei I* from *P. klugei II.* I had to wait no less than three days, for apparently the Customs Office did not know what to do with the shipment. But then the fish arrived.

I hurried home with them and started unpacking them. All fish were in good condition, except the bag that contained the *P. klugei II.* The trio, one male and two females, did not look too well. One of the females was dead, and the pair that was left were already swimming on their sides. I quickly placed the fish in a well-planted tank in the hope that they might recover. They really did, and the next day I was able to note their true colors. No resemblance to *P. klugei I* was noticed, neither in behavior nor in coloration. Contrasting with *P. klugei I*, the fish were of a much higher and sturdier build, and instead of the reddish-grey tint of *P. klugei I* they possessed a pretty yellow basic color, a real exception in the group *kribensis-taeniatus-subocellatus* of the genus *Pelmatochromis* which made me wonder about the name given to them.

I simply cannot imagine both "species" of *P. klugei* as being the same species. As far as I know, the name derives from Mr. Kluge, the Hamburg importer. Anyway, the species is very pretty and will surely find many people to fancy it. But let us get back to the fish.

My joy about them was pretty short-lived, for just a few days later the only one left was one solitary male. It is obvious that from then on I tried everything possible to get a new female. But I succeeded only two years later, this time in the form of ten young specimens which grew up quickly in my tank. They developed into four pairs, each of which I placed in a separate breeding tank. To my great astonishment, five days after the transfer all pairs spawned nearly simultaneously in the evening!

The breeding tanks I had set up were $7\frac{1}{2}$ gallon aquaria with the bottoms covered with fine-grained gravel. The tanks were densely planted and equipped with a flowerpot turned on its side. The water was simple tap water with a hardness of about 20°DH and a pH value of around 7. The temperature was 75°F. In each of the flowerpots the spawn was located on the right-hand upper wall. The eggs were of a pink color with an elongated oval shape. Their numbers varied between one hundred and one hundred and forty units.

I hoped to be able to let the parents care for their spawn. The consequence was that on the third day everything was fungused. From then on I decided to remove the flower-pots,

Both male and female, in non-spawning coloration, ignore each other.

As the female ventures near the cave of the male, she shows a completely different color pattern.

In full color, the pair enter the cave together during their "engagement" period.

The male guards the entrance to the cave as the female moves to the actual spawning site.

Turning so he can watch the female and guard the entrance to the cave at the same time, the male's colors heighten.

As spawning commences, the male tours the outside of the cave, even peeking underneath to insure that spawning is progressing satisfactorily.

with the eggs, from the breeding tanks, transferring them into smaller nursery tanks with filtration in which I had the clean, oxygen-enriched water circulate continuously over the spawnings. Excepting a few unfertilized eggs, everything hatched within three days. Four days later the fry were swimming free, so that I had to offer them their first food. For three days their fare were *Rotatoria*. Then I shifted the feeding over to *Cyclops* nauplii. On this diet, and with frequent changes of water, the young grew up quickly and reached a length of $1\frac{3}{8}$ inches after only three months.

Full-grown males reach a length of about four inches, the females always remaining $\frac{3}{4}$ of an inch smaller.

With regard to their home waters it should be added that *P. klugei II* stem from Nigeria where they are found in small streams with plenty of possibilities for hiding.

Some time ago I placed one pair of *P. klugei I* and two pairs of *P. klugei II* in a 48 inch-long tank. Each pair was provided with an overturned flower pot. The aquarium was neither overstocked nor understocked with plants, and richly ornamented with petrified wood.

All three pairs were put in simultaneously. The next day each pair had staked out its range and moved into a flower pot which was zealously defended. The *klugei II's* set up housekeeping at the two ends of the tank, while the *klugei I* had their establishment in the middle. A few days later one of the pairs of *klugei II* were in a matrimonial mood. In the evening they spawned, after the male and female had diligently cleaned the wall of the flower pot. The female lured the male into the pot, with her trembling body bent in front of him. This was done after she had already stuck a number of eggs to the wall. The male then entered the pot and fertilized the spawn while gliding over the eggs. Then he disappeared again. But he stayed in close vicinity to the pot, watching that no stranger might venture too near. If this happened the intruder was most quickly chased away. Now and then the male returned to the pot in order to further fertilize eggs the female had meanwhile stuck there.

After finishing the act of spawning the female took over the caring for the spawn, while the male went out on sentry duty in the surroundings of the flower pot.

This situation lasted two days. Then I noticed by the behavior of the other pair of *klugei II* at the other end of the tank, and by the bright red belly of the female, that here too the intent was spawning. Apparently I was not the only one to notice this fact! The first male, which had been watching the outskirts of the pot in which his female was, did so too. The colorful female at the other end made him forget his mate and his marital duties. He was unable to resist the temptation of seeing whether eventually he would not be needed there too . . . which evidently was not the case as there was already one male present! But our philandering male did not seem to notice this. He only had eyes for the pretty female. Maybe he just did not *want* to notice anything.

At first the male that really belonged was astonished at the audacity of the intruder and did not accept the situation complacently. What red-blooded he-man would? The female seemed quite pleased with the new male, though, and was already courting him intensively. Now the cuckolded male displayed his antagonism, but since he was a little weaker than the intruder he was finally forced to withdraw with folded fins. Anyone can imagine what his feelings were! He repeatedly tried to rout the intruder, but once more he was ignominiously routed by the homewrecker. Together with the female, the victorious usurper now cleaned the flower pot and spawning took place towards the evening.

Meanwhile the first wife of our Don Juan, which had kept caring for her spawn, noticed that her cherished husband had taken French leave. She searched everywhere to see where he was, but did not find him, as at the moment she searched he was inside the flower pot of his new mate.

The surroundings of the first flower pot were no more secure now, and the *P. klugei I* made their appearance in the

As soon as the female deposits a row of eggs, the male assumes the same inverted position and fertilizes them.

The female continues laying eggs

The female lays her eggs adjacent to each other. None of the eggs are laid one atop the other.

After spawning is completed the female signals the end by mouthing the eggs and removing any which are infertile.

The male, with his free-swimming fry, has taken on still another coat of coloration.

This is the time to watch the male. If his color heightens, he will almost surely eat his own spawn.

closest vicinity. The deserted female had quite some difficulty in blocking the inroads of the *P. klugei I,* but she did this most viciously so that the pair were forced to withdraw every time.

The next day the wife spotted her philandering husband, who now stood watch before the other flower pot! Lightning-like she rushed towards him, making quite a vicious attack. Her behavior clearly showed that she was angry and wanted to take him home again. This was repeated nearly the whole day, but without success on her side.

Like one of us humans, the deserted female finds the struggle for survival quite harder than before, especially if she has to provide for a flock of offspring. In order to save this female's sanity, for she had to continuously fight off the incursions of the *P. klugei I,* I siphoned off the newly hatched fry and reared them separately.

One day the female made the acquaintance of the vanquished male and they joined their destinies. Everything pointed towards a happy ending for those two victims of fate. For about 7 days they courted each other and spawning was to be expected at any moment. But, as the sage says: "Fate is a treacherous miscreant," and this came true again for our pair of *P. klugei II.* Mr. Casanova showed up again as soon as the female colored up, and the weaker male, who had gone to great efforts with the female, once more was permitted to watch from afar how his late conquest was being spawned.

In order not to be forced to watch the same spectacle over and over again, I took the male and the other female from the tank, transferring them to a smaller container where they have already spawned several times.

What I intend with this report is to point out that staring rapturously at a beautiful aquarium and its inhabitants is the lesser part of what our hobby has to offer. Only after you start paying attention to the behavior of your fishes will you be able to see the beauty and the miracles of nature.

As spawning time approaches for the oscar, their actions take a dramatic change. They swim to each other, but stop short with their mouths wide open. Other times they would spread their fins, extend their gill membranes and vibrate next to one another as shown here. Photo by Jukka Jarvi.

The Oscar

Astronotus ocellatus

It has been many years since I wrote the material in Book I of this series dealing with the oscar, and many new things have happened with this popular fish. First, I was successful in spawning the fish in large, outdoor pools in Florida. Of course the winters were too cold and one winter when the temperature of the water dropped to 55° all my oscars died! So from November to March, I move the oscar breeders inside in covered vats where the water rarely dipped below 70°. The oscar likes heat . . . even 90° suits him . . . but not 60°!

Trapping oscars in your outside pool is not easy. They don't enter the usual trap and if you try to seine them they dive right into the mud. Believe it or not, I removed my oscars from the pool using a barbless hook with a worm! It worked and I didn't kill a single fish.

In the spring, actually in late February, I drain a small pool say about 15 feet wide and 50 feet long, not deeper than four feet in the center, and lime it. The lime acts as a sterilizing agent and fertilizer and, after adding some cottonseed meal once the water has cleared, I wait for life

The pair soon select a spawning site which is usually a flat stone. A piece of bottom slate from a broken tank suits them perfectly. Photo by Jukka Jarvi.

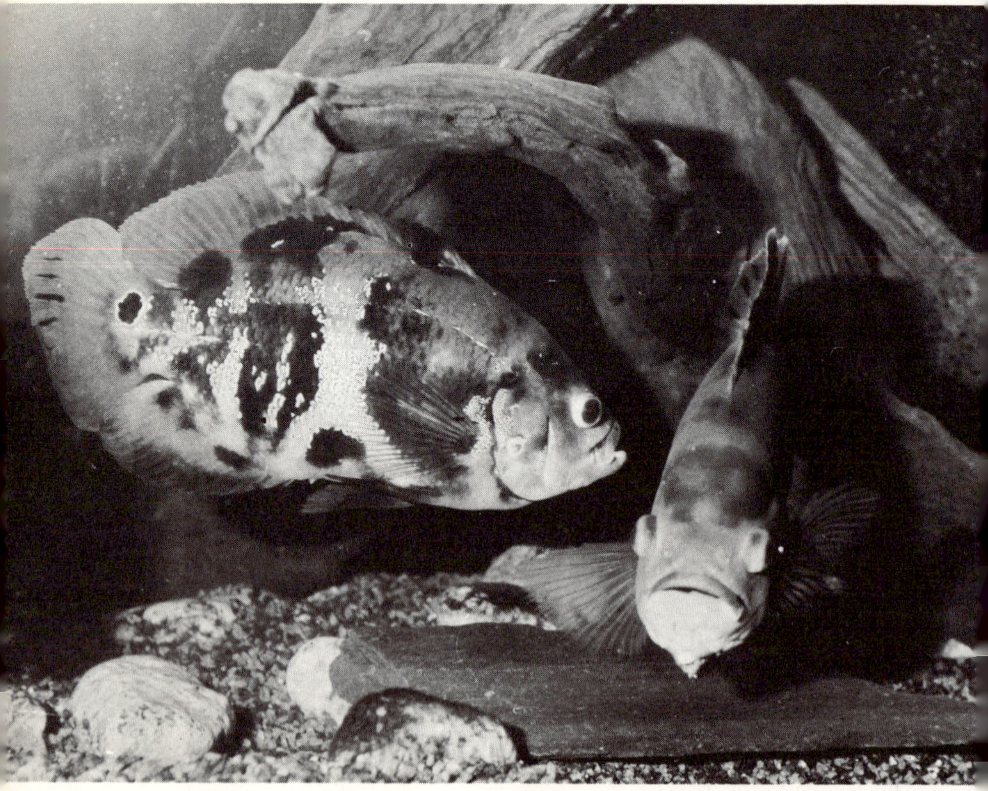

The red oscar. Photo by the author.

to appear in the form of *Daphnia* before I put in my oscars.

All around the bank, every five feet, I have a piece of slate with a hole drilled into it. The small hole is for a string so I can pull the slate out and examine it, or, if the water is clear enough for me to see the slate without pulling it out, I use the string to remove the slate when I spot a nest of eggs. Every morning I would walk around the pool and check the slates, removing those slates which had eggs on them. In this 15 × 50 feet pool I would keep about 20 large oscars about 12 inches long and during the breeding season from March to November, I would obtain about one spawning per month per pair of fish. With 12 pairs of oscars one year, I bred, raised and sold 320,000 fish one inch long. It was a very good year, as my average is more like 10,000 babies reaching selling size per pair of fish per year.

My oscars were very friendly and ate almost everything. Not only did I feed them crayfish, which they love and which, by the way, always stimulated them to spawn, but they ate frogs, tadpoles, pieces of dead birds that were shot eating our fish, pieces of snake and turtle, dried dog food pellets, mash and just about anything else that was high in protein. In Florida we had several thousand pools and each pool supported a colony of crayfish which we trapped and seined with the fish. The crayfish were too small to eat (about two inches long) but they tore the fish's fins as they pinched them when trapped with them, so we considered them a nuisance. We would collect a few hundred crayfish and throw them to the oscars. The oscars went wild for them and would grab them ferociously, crushing them in their strong jaws, obviously oblivious of their hard shells and sharp claws. They devour a dozen of them in as many minutes. Within 48 hours of a heavy feeding of crayfish, I also get 50% of the fish to spawn.

When the fish spawned in the pool, I merely removed the slate which contained the spawn and put it into a styrofoam shipping box right in the field, using the same water in which the fish spawned. I would then add about 20 drops of 5% methylene blue to the water and allow a stream of air from an airstone to play against the developing eggs very gently. As the eggs hatched, the young would hang from sticky head glands, falling softly to the bottom of the styrofoam box a few hours or days later. When all the fry had fallen to the bottom, I removed the slate and waited another few days for the helplessly wriggling mass of fry to become free swimming. The fish were very easy to see since they are so black (even the ones which will eventually turn red) and contrast so nicely with the white styrofoam. Then, too, I always used a new styrofoam box for each spawn and after it had been used I shipped fish in it, thus assuring myself of clean nurseries every time I need them. Of course I used these same styrofoam shipping boxes for all my

When cleaning the area, one of the fish would **S**-curve its body and dig viciously into the gravel as a cleaning action, perhaps to impress its mate. Photo by Jukka Jarvi.

Immediately before spawning, the pair would rub against each other with wide open mouths. Photo by Jukka Jarvi.

spawnings of tetras, cichlids and barbs, using the styrofoam box as a shipping container after it was once used as a spawning or nursery tank. Not only is it the cheapest tank available . . . it is the best since it is insulated and simply by using its own cover, the nursery tank temperature is maintained very uniformly . . . and it's always clean.

Back to the free swimming oscars . . . they are ravenously hungry as soon as they are free swimming, so I offer them freshly hatched brine shrimp which they gobble down. Feeding them five times a day is all they need to grow to $1\frac{1}{2}$ inches long in a month, when they must be sold. Of course it's much easier to raise the young in a large outside pool. Just treat the pool the same way it would have been set up for the breeders, sterilizing it with lime and fertilizing it with cow manure and cottonseed meal. When the pool is teeming with *Daphnia*, mosquito larvae and/or *Cyclops*, put in the free swimming fry and watch them grow. They grow more than twice as fast outdoors as they do in an aquarium.

If there is no flat rock available in the tank, the pair might dig a pit in the bottom sand until they reached something solid. These are young red oscars. Photo by the author.

As red oscars get older, they become more and more red. This fish is about one year old. Photo by the author.

In 1969 a red oscar appeared in Thailand. Never before have so many false rumors and misleading statements been made about an aquarium fish!

It has been said that the original breeder of the red oscar is anonymous. *He is not anonymous* and for the record, his name is Charoen Pattabongse and he lives at 189 Soi Sarasin, Raj Damri Road, Bangkok, Thailand. He breeds red oscars from male and female red oscars, though they do not always breed true, and if you breed a red oscar with any offspring of a red oscar, be it striped or not, it will produce red fish.

The fish are red or orange fairly early in life, certainly before they are six months old, but they do get redder as they get older.

In 1966 Charoen Pattabongse's only interest in fishes was to tend his beautiful goldfish on his magnificent estate almost in the center of Bangkok. About that time he decided to get some other fishes and after combing the local petshops, he decided to keep oscars and blue discus. His local dealer told him to select the oscars he wanted from a tank swarming with baby oscars, and Mr. Pattabongse's keen eye for beauty spotted a young fish which was much more colorful than his tankmates. He bought only one oscar and kept his eye open around Bangkok for another intensely colorful specimen.

Within a year his colorful fish grew to ten inches in length and had almost twice as much red as a normal male. One female, about eleven inches, caught his eye. She was very colorful, more colorful certainly than a normal female, but the owner wouldn't sell the fish, so Charoen borrowed her, agreeing to give the owner of the female a few hundred babies for her use.

He put the pair together in a circular concrete vat about thirty-nine inches in diameter and twenty inches deep. The first day the pair almost killed each other, but in April 1966, one month after he introduced the pair to each other, they spawned.

The fry numbered 1,600 when they were a month old and by feeding them heavily on fairy shrimp, he was able to make them show their red color at a very early age. He gave two hundred fry to the owner of the female and kept all the rest. Inasmuch as Charoen is not a professional breeder, he selected about ten extremely colorful fry and began a period of intensive selective inbreeding. In every generation he crossed the most colorful fish to each other until finally he got his all-red strain in early (March) 1969. During this time other breeders were using his rejected fish for their own breeding efforts, and they too produced some red fish.

Charoen Pattabongse is not an ordinary man. He is a

About 24 hours before spawning, the pair work intensively to clean the spawning site. Photo by Jukka Jarvi.

This female, with her ovipositor extending its full length, laid all the eggs shown before the male came over to spawn with her. Photo by Jukka Jarvi.

The male finally joins the female and they circle the spawning site; the male fertilizes the eggs as they are laid. Photo by Jukka Jarvi.

As soon as spawning is completed, the pair begin rough-housing it again, but they rarely do any serious damage to one another. The center of the spawn has been eaten by the male and represent the eggs laid by the female in his absence. Photo by Jukka Jarvi.

As the eggs develop, the pair hover over the eggs and fan them with their fins. Photo by Jukka Jarvi.

true nature-lover, and his garden not only contains bowls, pools and tanks full of fishes, but he has an unbelievable collection of Thai ornamental trees and orchids. The Thai trees were brought to Siam from Japan some two hundred years ago, when the Thai took the Japanese bonsai and teased them into symmetrical shapes. Charoen is an expert on these trees and it is this same eye for beauty and patience that led him into the development of the red oscar.

Charoen was a charming host when I visited him on February 19, 1970, and he was very proud to show me his blue discus, fancy goldfish and his large pool filled with red oscars. I hesitated to ask him for some of his breeding stock, but I finally worked up my courage and I was able to take two breeding pairs and an extra male, all about twelve inches long.

The Moonlight Gourami

Trichogaster microlepis

Southeast Asia, primarily Thailand, is the source and range of the moonlight gourami. I found my first specimens in Thailand in the early 1950's when I was collecting blood for soldiers in the Korean war. I found the moonlight gouramis while searching for Siamese fighting fishes, so you can picture me in shallow ditches mostly covered with vegetation that was being cultivated in the klongs (ditches or canals) by the Thai people.

While studying a ditch before I fished it, I always looked for telltale bubblenests. These bubblenests indicate that a gourami is in the neighborhood and is either getting ready

Young moonlight gouramis. Photo by G. J. M. Timmerman.

An immature female. Note that her snout is not yet turned up. Compare her profile with the fish in the spawning series. Photo by Ruda Zukal.

to breed or has already done so. It is very difficult to recognize the difference between various gourami nests and fighting fish nests in the wild, but the moonlight gourami is a bit special.

The moonlight gourami nest is a huge construction effort which contains large bits of vegetation amongst its thick, sticky bubbles. The moonlight gourami is not content to use dead or decaying leaves . . . he wants fresh leaves. I used the pronoun "he" without reservation, for the male does all the work in building the nest. Several authors, especially Hans Joachim Richter, have written about the tremendous effort that moonlight gouramis exert in building their nests. He describes (*Tropical Fish Hobbyist,* September, 1969) how

The female is the uppermost fish. She is slightly distended with eggs. The male is immediately below her. He is more slender and much more colorful. The photo below shows a closeup of the male. The upturned snouts are indications of sexual maturity. Photos by Hans Joachim Richter.

The male builds his nest amongst large leaves from aquatic vegetation. First, in the photo above, he floats leaves under the bubblenest. Then, photo below, he adds more bubbles to make the whole mass stick together. Photos by Hans Joachim Richter.

the fish tears out huge leaves of Amazon swordplants, cutting the leaves by constant sawing and biting. In the wild, the same plant-tearing operation can be observed, and when you see a nest with large leaves sticking out of it in all directions, you know that you have a moonlight gourami nest in view.

Why the moonlight gourami is so valuable is difficult to understand. It is a plain silvery fish without any highlights or markings at all. The stringy ventral fins may be red, and there may be a bit of red in the eye, but that's about all that breaks up the plain silver coloration. The moonlight gourami doesn't even have large silver scales whose edges and reflections could add drama to an otherwise colorless body! But it is one of my favorite fishes because it is so rare in nature and so difficult to breed for fishfarmers in Florida.

The moonlight gourami is as cool as moonlight. They are not passionate fish, and their breeding act lacks much of the vigor and sex-play that is so characteristic of most of the other gouramis. Once the male builds his nest, the fish spawn and that's it. But let me give you a step-by-step description so you can successfully breed the moonlight gourami . . . provided you have soft, slightly acid water.

If possible buy a dozen small fish which have been tank-bred. Almost all small fish are tank-bred, since the normal time for collecting this fish is during the dry season, long after breeding (most fishes breed during the beginning of the rainy season, when collecting is very difficult). Raise the fish together in as large an aquarium as possible. They do very well in a beautifully landscaped aquarium and they eat almost everything, though they favor floating foods, especially freeze-dried brine shrimp. If live *Tubifex* worms are offered they should be put into a feeding ring close to the surface of the water.

The fish eat heartily, and grow fast, almost an inch per month, if very well fed on all sorts of live and freeze-dried foods. Do not feed them frozen foods, as this fouls the tank and the most common frozen foods are 90% water, thus not nutritious enough for such fast-growing fish. Within about four months the fish should be breeding size, about four inches long. Soon you will notice that the females begin to show a fatter belly as their eggs begin to develop within their bodies. Every fat fish will usually be a female, while the slender fish, whose fins show a slight red coloration, may well be males.

Select the fattest female and the most slender, colorful male and place them into an aquarium which is very well planted with all sorts of bushy-leaved plants. (On occasions when I didn't have bushy-leaved plants I have successfully stuck leaves of spinach into the gravel and the moonlight male tore them out and made his nest of them!)

The pH of the water should be between 6.0 and 6.8, and the water should be as soft as possible. Rainwater is perfect, but add about 20% of the aquarium water in which the moonlights have been raised. Slowly raise the temperature to about 85°F. and soon you will see the male begin to build his nest. Leave the light on the aquarium all the time once you have placed the pair together. I use a long 20-gallon tank, 36 inches long, for breeding all gouramis. The bottom has an inch of sand, and the tank is well planted.

The male, once he has built his nest and thoroughly reinforced it with large plant leaves which he floats under the bubbles, will then bring the female under the nest to join him. He does this by swimming in front of her, spreading his fins and then swimming back to his nest. The fish face each other at about a 90° angle and then slowly the female approaches the male, well under the nest, and nestles into his folding body. They go through the handshake embraces and, as they slowly roll over, a large quantity of eggs are released. Spawning goes on for an hour or two; about 2,000 eggs are produced. The eggs slowly float to the surface, into and around the nest.

Those eggs which miss the nest are ignored. Neither the

The nest having been completed (above) the female is enticed and the usual spawning embrace occurs under the nest (photo below) during which thousands of eggs are released and float into the nest. Photos by Hans Joachim Richter.

The embrace of the moonlight gourami is the typical "handshake" type, where both fish wrap their bodies about each other. Photo by Hans Joachim Richter.

male nor the female pays any attention to either the eggs or the nest once spawning has been accomplished. The eggs all hatch within 24 hours at the high spawning temperature, and the fry are free-swimming in 72 hours after spawning. I usually remove the parents after spawning, as they have very little interest in preserving or helping the young.

Once the fry are free-swimming the problem begins, for the fry require copious amounts of newly prepared infusoria, especially rotifers. They must be fed at least every half hour, so allow the culture to continuously drip into the aquarium so that feeding is constant. Once the fry take newly hatched brine shrimp (which may be one to two weeks after they hatch), their growth will be rapid. These fish eat more than any other gourami fry I have had experience with, and they grow one inch per month if they have all the food they require. Squeezed egg yolk is well appreciated . . . but be careful not to foul the aquarium.

A pair of striped gouramis. The male, to the left, is larger and more colorful than the female. Photo by G. J. M. Timmerman.

The Striped Gourami

Colisa fasciata

Most of the smaller gouramis in the genus *Colisa* are popular and well known. They all have peaceful habits and beautiful colors. Most of them are easy to spawn. There are, however, two species which are not quite the same as the others, *Colisa labiosa* and *Colisa fasciata*. Both of these species are pugnacious and aggressive. Both are sexually aggressive towards their own and other gourami females, and males are easily spawned with females of other *Colisa* species.

I think that both *Colisa fasciata* and *Colisa labiosa* are more closely related than two species in the same genus. I think they are the same species, possibly subspecies. They freely interbreed, though this is not proof they are related. For purposes of discussion, I will differentiate between the

Pre-spawning sex play includes, on very rare occasions in gouramis, mouth-locking. Photo by Hilmar Hansen, Aquarium Berlin.

A pair of old striped gouramis. The male, lower fish, has a lump on his head which is typical of gouramis almost two years old and probably too old to spawn. The female, also very old, shows a slight lump, but she is obviously not filling with eggs. Photo by Günter Senfft.

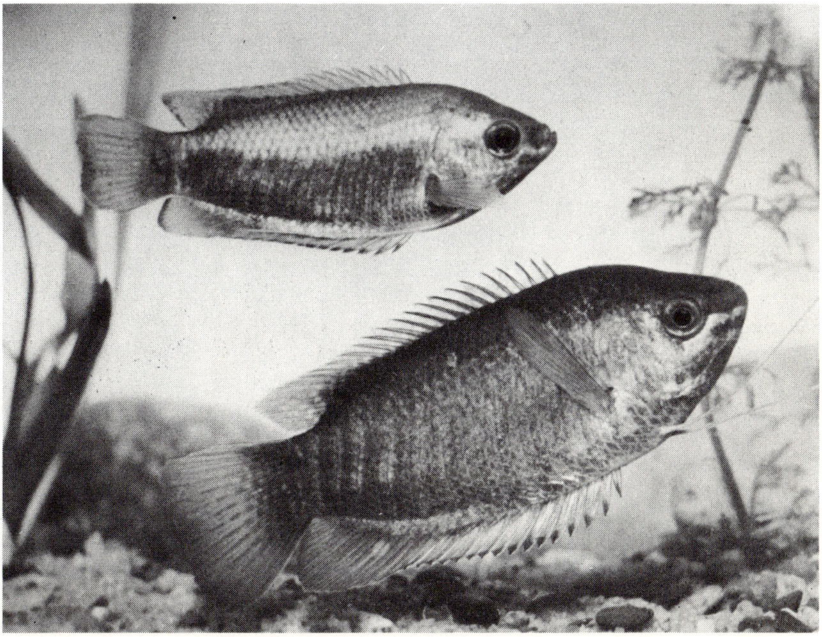

Both male and female in full color, the female gently bites the male, indicating her willingness to spawn. This leads to a spawning embrace (photo below) which usually takes place under the bubblenest. Photos by Hans Joachim Richter.

Not all embraces result in eggs and there are several false starts, or dry runs as they are sometimes called. When eggs finally are produced (lower photo), they float gently up into the nest. It is rare that the pair sink to the bottom, as is shown here, during their embrace. Photo by Hans Joachim Richter.

two "species" by defining as *C. labiosa* that fish which has a red edge on the dorsal of the male while *C. fasciata* has a white edge on the male's dorsal fin during spawning.

Reports of the pugnaciousness of the fish known as *C. fasciata* are legend. They attack large cichlids and lock jaws with them; they spawn with any gourami female in the same tank. They tear females to shreds if they won't spawn. All true! Here's how you may go about spawning this beautiful fish, should you find some available.

Keep the male separate in a long 20-gallon aquarium which is heavily planted. Feed him very well on live foods and freeze-dried foods. The females can be kept together in much smaller tanks, as they don't fight under normal circumstances. With water which has a slightly acid pH, from 6.0 to 6.8, in very soft condition, the male should begin to color up after a few weeks of good feeding. The females should also fatten up as their color begins to grow more and more intense. Once the female grows a bit fat (don't wait too long or she might become eggbound), she may be placed in with the male.

The male might attack her once or twice, but he usually doesn't do any serious damage. Once he ascertains that she is a female and available, he begins the construction of a very poor bubblenest only a few bubbles deep. He normally doesn't weave any debris or plants into the nest but gets the job over with as quickly as possible. Then he poises himself under the nest and awaits the female's arrival. Usually as soon as she comes near the nest he attacks her, probably tearing her fins a bit at this stage. After several attempts at spawning, the female is finally rewarded and induces the male to embrace. Their embrace is the typical "handshake," with the male wrapping about the female, squeezing the eggs from her as he fertilizes them. Often the first few attempts at embrace are awkward and do not result in the production of any eggs. These mock matings are normal and usual.

A male in typical good coloration. This is a young male as evidenced by the straight profile of the head. Photo by Hilmar Hansen, Aquarium Berlin.

Once the eggs are squeezed from the female, she remains dormant for a short time, seemingly paralyzed, and then hides from the male, who seeks out the floating eggs and blows them into a unified mass in the center of his nest. This process is repeated several times until one to two thousand eggs have been laid and the male has blown them into a large yellow mass in his scrawny bubblenest.

As the pair repeat their spawning act, the male seems more and more tired, and the partners often sink and hit the bottom of the tank as they embrace. The female always "plays dead" after the embrace and gives the male a chance to get the eggs before she races away to hide, only to come after the male to spawn again in a few minutes.

The spawning continues all day until the female is unable to produce any more eggs . . . nevertheless she continues spawning. In the wild the male probably chases her away. In the aquarium it would be wise to remove both breeders at this time or else remove the eggs and the female.

As the pair finish spawning, the male immediately searches for the eggs and, using his mouth as a catch-all, blows them into the nest. The female usually remains stunned after the embrace and lays as though dead (upper photo). The male gathers all the eggs together and tends the nest as best he can. As he moves about the nest, the eggs are fanned by his movements and swirl about him. Photos by Hans Joachim Richter.

A male in superb, but non-spawning coloration.

I use a large soup dish to remove the eggs merely by slipping the plate under the nest. The floating eggs go right into the dish and can be placed into a large, very shallow aquarium where they may be raised without any trouble.

The eggs hatch in a day at 80°F. and with a thousand or more fry, you should have a huge supply of the finest infusoria available. Rotifers are the best first food for all baby gouramis, so have a few of those cultures going (get instructions from your local high school biology teacher if your petshop can't help you). After a few weeks you can switch to newly hatched brine shrimp and egg yolk, after which growth is more rapid.

These are indeed beautiful fishes and will become more popular once they have been spawned in Florida by the pool farmers.

A pair of blue gularis. The male, to the right, is much more colorful than the drab female. It is frequently difficult to visually identify females of various species of killifish. Photo by Ruda Zukal.

The Blue Gularis

Aphyosemion sjoestedti

William T. Innes, in his monumental work *Exotic Aquarium Fishes,* was responsible for the education of most aquarists during the formative period of the hobby between 1920 and 1950. He was also responsible for some terribly misleading identifications (unintentionally, of course) and this fish is probably one of the best examples. For many years every writer and aquarist called the blue gularis either *Aphosemion coeruleum* or *A. gularis,* names given it by Innes. Even today, in Innes' hopelessly outdated book (Innes died at the age of 93), no one has bothered to change the name of this fish to *A. sjoestedti.*

My fondness for this fish dates back to 1958, when I spent a month trying to find it! I never did find it in Africa, in the Cameroons where Sjöstedt said he discovered it, nor

The male, noticing the ripe, plump female (above) directs his attention to her and tries to force her to the bottom where they will deposit their eggs. Photos by Ruda Zukal.

A tank-raised male blue gularis photographed in 1969 by the author.

The photo, by William T. Innes, which was erroneously identified by Innes as *Aphyosemion coeruleus*, and confused aquarists for 30 years.

did anyone else that I know of. J. J. Scheel in his authoritative book *Rivulins of the Old World* (T.F.H., 1968, pp. 400-407, first edition) describes in great detail the scientific classification of this fish. Read his book if you have any interest in killifish at all. It is probably the best book ever written on a group of fishes.

Like most *Aphyosemion* the males of this species are much more colorful and have much more exotic finnage than do the females. If these were birds, we would be told that the female is protectively colored since she must sit on the eggs and remain camouflaged while a predator might be in the neighborhood. The same thing may not be true for fishes, especially for the *Aphyosemion* species since they show no post-spawning care of the young or the eggs.

As the male jockeys the female closer and closer to the bottom of the aquarium, he begins to line himself up alongside her. In the photo below, the male takes a spawning position alongside the female . . .

. . . but the female has other ideas and she eludes the male, obviously not being ready to spawn. The male quickly pursues her and starts all over again. Photos by Ruda Zukal.

The blue gularis is not a fish for the beginner. It is a fish for someone who wants to be famous in his own area. With just a little bit of practice and patience, the fish can be maintained in comfort and bred in quantity, and without too much trouble you can be the person supplying all the baby blue gularis in your area . . . at very high prices!

Since the blue gularis male grows to about $5\frac{1}{2}$ inches long and is pugnacious, each male must be kept separately in his own breeding aquarium. I use 10-gallon aquariums which have a small flowerpot with a few *Cryptocoryne* plants in them. Since this fish can be kept alive only with live foods, I use *Tubifex* worms and baby guppies. The worms drop to the bottom of the tank where the blue gularis prefers to stay. Since I have no gravel at the bottom, I have no problem with fouling of the water. I do not use a heater or

A young male gularis. Photo by Dr. Herbert R. Axelrod.

a filter. The fish does well at temperatures between 62° and 75°, which is roughly room temperature. I spawn the male every few months and I use two or three females with each male.

The male's tank is converted to a breeding tank by the addition of spawning mops to the bottom. These spawning mops are of boiled green nylon, of the type used for knitting. I have also used bushy plants, and while I was first studying the fish, I often observed them spawning right into the sand. The fish are definitely bottom spawners. Since you can keep as many females together as you need, say 15 of them in a 10-gallon aquarium, they present little problem. They, too, require lots of live food in the form of worms, small fishes, flies, brine shrimp or *Daphnia*. Feed them as much and as often as possible. As they fill with roe, they will get fatter and fatter. Don't isolate them too long once they fill with roe or they may well become eggbound. Once a female is eggbound, she is worthless. Often, when placed with the male, she will be killed in the spawning effort.

Once the male has been well fed for a month and you have a few full females, introduce them into the aquarium of the male. They should start spawning within an hour, with the male chasing the females about the tank until he finally forces one of them into the sand where they drop, perhaps bury, a few eggs. Spawning goes on continually, for days or weeks, but egg production slowly drops from about 20 eggs per day per female to 2 or 3, when the females should be removed.

The advantage of the nylon mop becomes evident at this stage, for it can easily be removed from the aquarium, gently squeezed dry, and the clear eggs are easily seen and felt. The good eggs are tough, so don't worry too much about breaking

The spawning trio which were photographed in black and white for the accompanying photo series. Photo by Ruda Zukal.

The four photographs on these pages show the male successfully . . .

. . . forcing the female into spawning position at the bottom of the tank.

Ooops . . . she slipped (photo above), but the next time (photo below) he gets her lined up, and finally forces her into the sand where a few eggs are expelled (top facing page). As they break their embrace, the female recovers quickly (bottom facing page).

Often the male gets involved with both females at once. This almost invariably ends in no eggs being produced as the male is only capable of forcing one female into the bottom at a time. When he is faced with two females, he will select one (lower photo) and spawn with her. Photo by Ruda Zukal.

After spawning is complete, the female looks much more slender. Photo by Ruda Zukal.

them. Pick out the eggs carefully with tweezers or with your fingernails and place them into some damp peat moss. Or you can even leave them in the wet nylon mop. I separate them, count them, placing about 25 eggs into a cotton bag filled with damp peat moss which has been boiled and cooled. I then write the date on the bag and place all the bags into a large plastic bag which keeps the temperature more constant and maintains the dampness. Both breeders and eggs like darkness, so don't keep either exposed to the sun. After six weeks, drop the eggs into small, all-glass aquaria and remove the hatched out fry every day. 75% of the eggs should hatch in two weeks. By heavily feeding the fry on newly hatched brine shrimp, they grow to three inches long in three months and will start breeding themselves. The lack of a constant food supply will stunt their growth, but they will spawn anyway.

While I have little difficulty in breeding these fish, some people do. Several breeders suggest the addition of a pound of salt (sea salt or "kosher" salt is preferable) to 100 gallons of water, to make the fish feel more comfortable. The whole trick with breeding the blue gularis is a constant supply of live foods. In the wild they are probably insect feeders.

When I caught these fish in Brazil, I thought they were two males. The top fish is the male, the bottom fish (note the spot in the dorsal fin) is a female. Photo by the author.

The Red-Spotted Copeina

Copeina guttata

During my many expeditions to Brazil I have never failed to capture large quantities of the various *Copeina-Copella* fishes because they are always so easy to catch. Normally I find them in a relatively isolated pond that looks very shallow. Usually the area looks like something that has recently been flooded, since grass seems to be growing from the banks right into the water. This type of situation seems to bring *Copeina* species into my net . . . all the *Copeina* species, that is, except *Copeina guttata*. Why is that? *Because they like sandy bottoms.*

Don't be fooled by these two fish. They are two males. The male has a less intense dorsal spot when not spawning. Photo by the author.

The male, in the photo above, displays in front of the female. As soon as he attracts her attention, he will force his body against hers (photo below). Photos by Ruda Zukal.

Since his motive is to get the female to the bottom where they will spawn in a pit, the male does everything possible, including biting (upper photo) to get the female to the bottom reaches of the tank. Photos by Ruda Zukal.

No! Not a pair, but two males! Photo by the author.

A pair ready for spawning. The male has the clear dorsal fin. Photo by Ruda Zukal.

A plump male ready for spawning. Note the unmarked dorsal fin. Below is a photograph of a female, just as colorful as the male, but with a dark spot in her dorsal. Photos by Ruda Zukal.

Part of the pre-spawning play is the biting of each other's body. The male bites the female in the upper photo, while the female bites the male in the lower photo.

After the biting is finished, the male digs the pit and the pair proceed (lower photo) to lay their eggs in the depression. Series of photos by Ruda Zukal.

Copeina is not a consistent genus from the point of view of the habits of the fishes in it. They all seem to have very different ways to breed. *Copeina arnoldi* likes to lay eggs out of the water, splashing them to keep them wet. Most of the other *Copeina* merely deposit a few eggs at random locations and pay absolutely no attention to them (except perhaps to eat them). *Copeina guttata* digs a pit and spawns in it.

In order to spawn the red-spotted copeina, I suggest that you get as large an aquarium as possible up to 20 gallons. Look for a pair of fish in good condition and place them into the spawning tank, separated by a tank divider. The tank should contain freshly "aged" water with a pH below 7.2 and above 6.0 with as little hardness as possible. A well

As they begin to spawn in their depression . . .

. . . the fish line up alongside each other. Zukal photos.

planted aquarium with a deep sandy bottom is preferred. The center area should be kept clear of vegetation so the fish can dig their depression in which to deposit their eggs.

Males are easily recognized by their reddish fins and the bright red spots along their sides. The ocellus (eye-spot) in the dorsal fin of the males is much less intense than the homologous spot in the female's dorsal fin. The female is smaller, as well, and has almost no red spots on her side. The fish have top-opening mouths similar to killifishes and, of course, none of the *Copeina* or *Copella* species has an adipose fin, as do most of the other characins.

After feeding the two fish well for a few weeks, slowly raise the water temperature to 80°; if the temperature is around 80° to begin with, then raise it 5° more than it was.

First the fish jockey for position in the depression in which their eggs will be laid.

Then the male lies inside the slight depression as the female comes to join him. Photos in this series by Ruda Zukal.

The female squeezes under the male to lay her eggs in the upper photo, while the pair expel eggs into the depression in the lower photo.

The large male fertilizing the eggs as the female lays them in the depression in the sand. Photo by Ruda Zukal.

The male should soon begin to color up, with his anal fin taking on a brilliant yellow-red. When this happens you should remove the partition and allow the pair to spawn. If the fish are primed properly, spawning should take place within a few hours . . . oftentimes it takes place within a few minutes! Spawning is preceded by the usual sex play with the male and female chasing each other and tantalizingly rubbing against each other's body as they swim through the tank.

The male, in the interim, has fanned and mouthed a depression in the sand; his object seems to be to force the female into that depression. After a few rapid tremblings in mid-water, the female eventually follows the male into the pit, and they drop their almost invisible eggs into the depression.

Even as the pair spawn, the male may continually dig out the depression. Photo by Ruda Zukal.

Spawning continues, with almost invisible, tiny eggs being deposited in the depression in the sand. Photos by Ruda Zukal.

This act is repeated for hours until the male finally stops chasing the female and begins to guard and fan the eggs in cichlid fashion. Leave the male with the eggs for a day, then remove him as soon as the eggs hatch. Normally at 80° the eggs hatch in 36 hours. I have successfully hatched the eggs without the male by using an airstone one inch above the eggs. The fry remain as a wriggling mass in the depression for another three days until they finally become free swimming.

The female should have been removed immediately after spawning. The male should have been removed immediately after the young hatch or are free swimming. Often the male will eat the eggs, the developing young, or the free-swimming young. Hatching the babies without the father is not dangerous at all.

The male will chase the female away as soon as spawning is compete and he will guard and aerate the nest. The dorsal spot returns to the male after spawning is complete, but this spot is never as intense as that of the female.

The temperature must be kept high for the babies. Never allow it to fall below 80° or the babies seem to die.

The fry develop fast but require copious amounts of very fine infusoria for the first week of their lives until they are able to take newly hatched brine shrimp, about ten days after they are free-swimming. Once they begin taking this nourishing food, they should be able to grow half an inch every month until in about one year they will have reached their maximum size of about 5½ inches for males.

The red-spotted copeina is a very peaceful fish and makes a valuable addition to the community aquarium. Don't pass them up when you see them in your petshop.

Sexing head and tail light tetras is easy if the fish are mature. In the photo on the facing page (by Zukal), the male is the lower fish; in the Stanislav Frank photo above, the female is the upper fish. This female is probably egg-bound and will perish within a day or so. If females become too heavy with eggs and they have no chance of spawning, they usually die.

The Head and Tail Light Tetra

Hemigrammus ocellifer

From Guyana and the Amazon waters comes a very beautiful fish which hobbyists have known since 1910. The head and tail light tetra was at one time the most popular characin kept in aquariums. It was hardy, easy to breed and easy to sex. Its popular name resulted from the obvious glow coming from reflected light in the eye and caudal peduncle. It is interesting that in every language (Spanish, Swedish, German, Dutch, Czech, Hungarian and Russian) this fish is called the head and tail light tetra.

A ripe pair (above), with the male very slim, active and colorful, while the female is heavy, with full finnage. Below, two females approach a male. Two females were used with one male in this photo sequence by Ruda Zukal.

The pair of head and tail light tetras head for the bushes as this is where they will spray their eggs. Photo by Ruda Zukal.

The head and tail light tetra is a community aquarium fish. It gets along well with all kinds of fishes, whether or not they are tetras. If you are lucky enough to be able to buy a school of them, say 20 to 30, for a 20-gallon aquarium, you'll get greater pleasure when they school together, but if you can only afford a pair, you'll find pleasure even if they are housed in a 2-gallon aquarium. Usually males never get larger than $1\frac{1}{2}$ inches, the females growing a bit larger.

I was able to condition my breeders in water at 74°F. It was necessary to feed them freeze-dried foods to supplement the normal dried foods.

I had no difficulty in breeding these beautiful fish. I selected a trio of two females and one male. Most people said I should have used two males to one female . . . but all I had was one male. I placed them into a 5-gallon aquarium

As the pair head for the bushes, the male suddenly swerves into the female (upper photo) and she twists her body as though to avoid him. At the moment of collision, eggs are expelled and fertilized (lower photo). Photos in this series by Ruda Zukal.

The pair repeatedly head for the planted parts of the aquarium and collide, with one fish poking the other in the side, at which time eggs are released and fertilized.

This exceptional sequence of three photos (see facing page), shows the trio of head and tail light tetras group spawning amongst the fine-leaved plants. Their spawning activity seems to be limited to collisions and bumpings against one another at which time the tiny eggs are expelled and stick to the plants. Except for possibly eating their eggs, the breeders pay no further attention to them. Photos by Ruda Zukal.

As spawning continues, for hours . . .

which was heavily planted with fine-leafed plants which you can easily see from the photos. I slowly raised the temperature of the tank to 82° with a thermostatic heater. All that was necessary was to turn the thermostat screw about half a turn every few hours; in 4 hours the tank was at the desired temperature and the resultant temperature increase was enough stimulation.

I experimented previously with a plain aquarium. This time I used a sand bottom. Both times I had excellent spawns so I conclude that you can use either a normally planted aquarium with sand, or a bare tank. I prefer sand so I can use an underground filter. In this way I can raise the young in the same tank in which the eggs are laid since the undergravel filter doesn't suck in babies the way other filters do. My breeders were about a year old, but the females were able to lay eggs at an earlier age than the males were able to fertilize them.

Sexing head and tail light tetras is simple. Besides the obvious difference in size, the females are thicker and their air bladder is invisible through their bodies. The males are slender and their bodies are more transparent so the air bladder is more visible.

To induce the fish to spawn, I first placed the male in the aquarium alone. This was done in the evening. Early the next day I put in the two females. Then I started to raise the temperature of the aquarium water. That same day they started spawning.

Spawning was typical of most tetras. The female dashed into the plants and the male followed her. The male then spread all his fins, especially his pectoral fins, and the female seemed to line herself up with these fins so that most spawning took place with the fish's eyes lined up. Then the

. . . the fish keep colliding and releasing eggs.

This series of three photographs (see facing page 192) shows further spawning activity as the trio become more and more involved in their spawning frenzy. Head-to-side attacks are more rare, as body-slapping, side-to-side, becomes the fashion. Photos by Ruda Zukal.

fish would squirm against each other with repeated S-curving. The female always started the S-curving for some reason. After a few spawnings, the females started following the males into the water plants and after two hours spawning activity ceased. Eggs were scattered all over the plants.

Soon the fish started to eat their own spawn and easily brushed the scattered eggs about so much that many fell to the bottom of the aquarium. Naturally I quickly removed the breeders.

In two days the eggs had all hatched and when the young were free swimming I offered them Fry Treet and loose pack freeze-dried brine shrimp. I raised about 160 from this spawn.

The diamond tetra gets its name from the reflective scales along the sides of both males and females. The males (above and on the facing page) were photographed with front lighting (above) and top lighting (facing page) to give the reader some idea of how the fish got its name "diamond tetra" from the way it sparkles under almost any kind of lighting.

The Diamond Tetra

Moenkhausia pittieri

In many instances the local hero (*fish* in this case) is never recognized as such, but is hailed in foreign lands. In my own New Jersey I have never seen any local black-banded sunfish in any of the local aquarium stores; in Germany I have never seen any store that didn't have black-banded sunfish. The opposite experience was true in Caracas, Venezuela when, during the spring, 1971 I found several petshops selling tropical fish and all of them had specimens of the very beautiful diamond tetra which comes from their own Lake Valencia region.

These four spawning photographs (see facing page also) illustrate the male spreading his fins in display before the female as he attempts to lead her into the darkened part of the aquarium where they will spawn. Photos by Ruda Zukal.

Diamond tetras are peaceful, colorful and hardy. They make wonderful additions to the community aquarium.

Even immature specimens of the diamond tetra are interesting especially if kept in dark water with as little light as possible.

As the diamond tetra spawns, eggs are scattered all about the aquarium. Tiny amber eggs are sprayed in every direction as the pair bump into each other, releasing sperm and eggs with each collision. On the facing page, the pair are seen going through the usual spawning gymnastics. The eggs are too small to be seen. Photos by Ruda Zukal.

This fish is not popular as a pet. I have never seen it in any of the many fish shows I judge every year, nor have I seen many of them offered for sale in petshops. If you ever see any, buy them as they are amongst the most beautiful of all aquarium fishes when kept under ideal circumstances. What are these ideal circumstances?

They require water which is slightly acid and hard. This may take a bit of doing but it usually happens when the gravel in the aquarium has stones which dissolve in the water. Mineral water of any type is usually useful (even if you have to buy it by the small bottle), so check the labels of the mineral waters from natural springs which may be offered by your local supermarket. See if the pH is neutral to slightly acid (7.0 to 6.6). That's the kind of water you want. Set up a nicely planted tank in as dark an area as possible, use very little light except when you want to see your pets, and you'll be amazed at the greenish, golden sparkling beauties the diamond tetras will become. Keep them alone, as many as possible in one aquarium. They do not require very warm water, 70°F. will do, but it should be warmed up to 80° to induce spawning.

Spawning is simple and will take place regularly unless you separate the sexes with a tank divider. A male will chase a female into the thickets and they will rub, bump and squeeze each other as they squirt semi-adhesive eggs against

A ripe female diamond tetra (upper fish), has shorter and less pointed fins than the male (lower fish). Photo by Dr. Stanislav Frank.

the plants. The tiny amber eggs may number 200 for a large, extremely heavy female and the eggs hatch in about one day at 80°. Within a week, maybe six days, the young are free swimming and very hungry. They must be fed infusoria immediately, with copious amounts of newly hatched San Francisco brine shrimp available a few days later. If they don't eat the brine shrimp it means their mouths are still too small for this sized food and you must use other plankton (infusoria). Of course the parents must be separated from the young and the eggs as soon as spawning has occurred or they will devour them instantly.

This is a worthwhile fish and one to be recommended for the specialist breeder who wants to earn money with his hobby.

A pair of green rivulus. The male has the colorful tail. Photo by Ruda Zukal.

Guyana Green Rivulus

Rivulus holmiae

All I remember about my first visit to British Guiana in 1954 (called Guyana now) was green. The jungle was complete and covered over everything until we got close to Georgetown and I knew there had to be many interesting fishes to be found with so much jungle . . . which means so much rain . . . which means so many streams . . . which means so much food for the fishes.

In a few hours I had comfortably settled into a nice hotel, put on my sneakers and hired a taxi for a ride. I never go anywhere without a small net and a bottle, so when we

This sequence of four photographs shows the male "slapping" the female with his body, finally forcing her into *Nitella* in which they will deposit their eggs. Photos by Ruda Zukal.

came to our first stream very close to the sea, I asked the driver to stop. I then dug amongst the soft plants for my first catch.

I was disappointed that day, almost everywhere I fished and looked, all there was to be found were guppies. Then I spotted a small quiet puddle in which something moved as indicated by the rings diverging and getting ever wider

During the spawning process, the pair always stay very close together, even when they are not actually laying eggs. Photo by Ruda Zukal.

on the still surface. Was this a fish or a frog?

It was a beautiful male *Rivulus holmiae*, about three inches long, which was bright green; greener than any fish I had ever seen . . . as green as a banana leaf. Its yellow tail margins on the top and bottom accentuated the blue-green of the inner part of the tail. I was terribly impressed with

While spawning, the pair line themselves up, parallel to each other, as seen in this excellent top view of a spawning pair by Ruda Zukal.

this green *Rivulus* and fished the whole area until I had collected about 30 fish. A few days later they arrived in New York where they would be kept until I got back a few weeks later.

Upon my return home I inquired about the fish and was told that there were only five left. It seemed that the first night they were put into a 20-gallon aquarium which was carelessly covered with a screen top, the usual thing utilized in wholesale fish rooms where the top is continually removed. A small crack in one corner was all the fish needed to jump out. Every fish had jumped out but five had jumped into other tanks rather than onto the floor where they dried out and died.

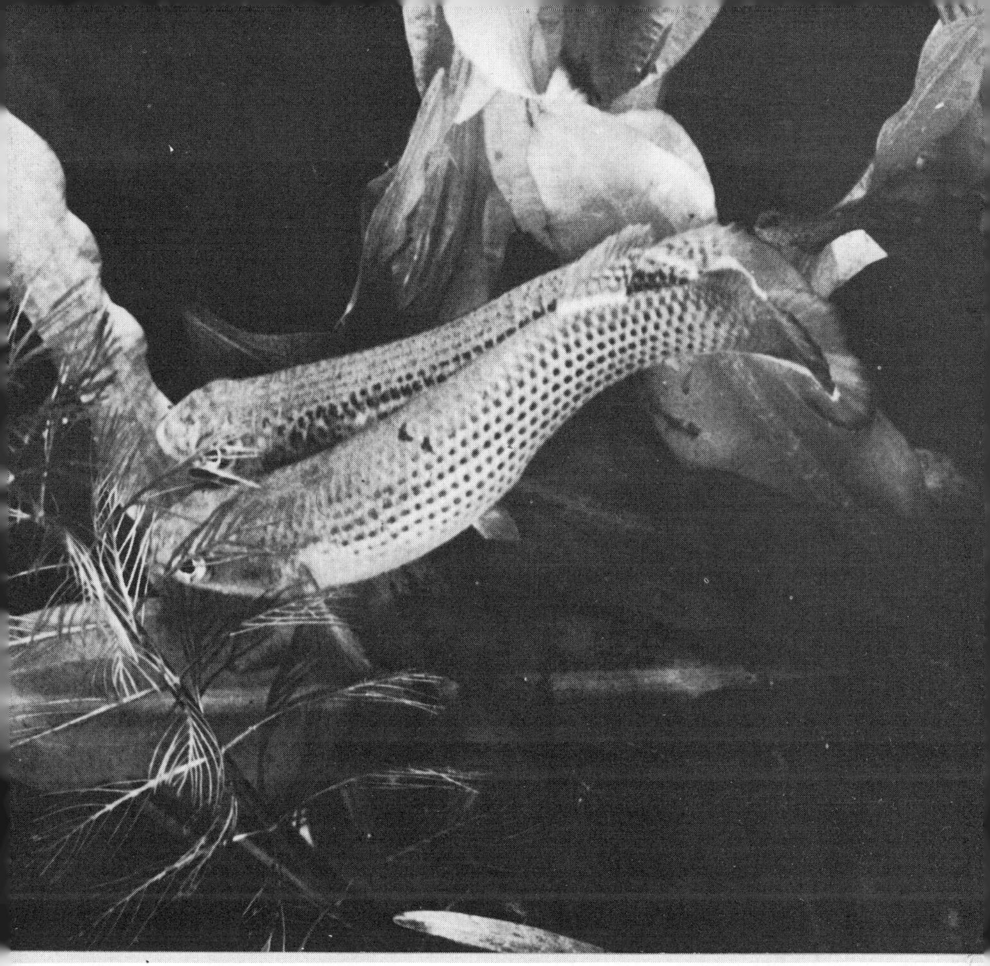

The three photos, above and facing page, show the pair spawning in bottom plants (top, facing page), in the sand (bottom, facing page) and in mid-water on a fine-leaved plant. Photos by Ruda Zukal.

These beautiful fish, which I call "Guyana greens," are very easy to care for. They are not too particular about their water. I keep them in moderately hard water, some salt added, at a temperature of about 78°. Their tank is heavily laden with artificial spawning grass (available at your petshop), and every week or two I merely pick out the grass and look for the large eggs which are stuck fast. There is no rush in looking for the eggs since they take a few weeks to hatch anyway, and they don't dry out during the

The photo above, and those on the facing page, show the Guyana green actually spawning. The pair remain very close to each other as the eggs are extruded a few at a time over a long period of time. Photos by Ruda Zukal.

short time they are exposed to the air while you are searching for them. I use about ten males and five females in a five-gallon aquarium for breeding and I leave them together for a few weeks at a time. Then I separate the sexes, feed them heavily and, as soon as the females fatten up, I put the fish together once again.

The parents usually don't bother the eggs if they are well fed on live foods, especially *Tubifex* worms, but they usually will eat their own free-swimming babies.

The fry grow very fast once they have been hatched in small hatching trays and offered newly hatched brine shrimp as soon as they have absorbed their yolk sacs. They are very hardy and grow rapidly.

A male dwarf chameleon fish displaying in front of his flowerpot cave, trying to woo a female into the cave to spawn. Photo by Ruda Zukal.

Dwarf Chameleon Fish

Badis badis badis

From India, Burma and Thailand come three different subspecies of a very interesting little fish which acts like a cichlid and a leaf fish, spawns like a cichlid and gourami and

So successful was the male that he ended up with two females, and the battle begins. All three fish fight amongst themselves to see which of the two females will spawn. Even if there were only a pair of fish, fighting would be still part of the spawning ritual. Photos by Ruda Zukal.

tetra, and changes colors like a chameleon. If you would really like to try your hand at a very interesting fish, with almost guaranteed results, get yourself a few pair of *Badis*, put them into a five-gallon aquarium, feed them heavily for a few weeks on live foods and I can almost guarantee they will spawn. Of course there are a few other things that are necessary, like a thermostatic heater to raise the temperature, an undergravel filter to keep the water clean and the temperature uniform, and a cave!

Setting up your aquarium for spawning any of the subspecies of *Badis* should be predicated upon the desire for

The pair of fish circle each other, with slow movements and extended finnage, until they attack. Photo by Ruda Zukal.

A male chameleon fish in non-spawning coloration. Color varies with diet, attitude and background coloration. Photo by Hilmar Hansen, Aquarium Berlin.

absolute privacy for each male in the tank. Caves formed by rocks, or partially buried flowerpots, should be so arranged that there is one for each male. The entranceway can be small or large, with a front and/or back door. The male will usually occupy the cave at all times, except when looking for a mate or when feeding. The female, on the other hand, seems to be continually scrounging for food.

The battle starts with the male, the darker fish, attacking the female (upper photo). Below, the pair lock jaws and thrash about vigorously. Photos by Ruda Zukal.

After briefly, but thoroughly, fighting, the pair circle each other in gourami fashion and prepare for a spawning embrace. Prior to this, their spawning behavior was almost typically cichlid. Photos by Ruda Zukal.

As the female fattens up, the male will spend more and more time courting her, until finally he woos her into his cave. The venturesome female that might try to enter the cave without an invitation from the male will be vigorously ejected!

As the female fattens up, the water conditions should be checked to ascertain that the water is normally hard (from 30 to 85 ppm.), with a temperature anywhere in the 70's. To accelerate spawning, I raise the temperature to about 85° and almost immediately the male begins to become more colorful.

A related subspecies is *Badis badis burmanicus*, from Burma. This male is in typical non-spawning coloration. Photo by the author.

The various color phases run from a pale brown fish that is frightened, to a very colorful red and blue checkered pattern which can be seen in the accompanying color photographs. Unfortunately the male only has color during spawning or when he becomes acclimated to an aquarium and has his private cave. In petshops where fish must be

A female *Badis badis burmanicus* in non-spawning coloration. Photo by Hilmar Hansen, Aquarium Berlin.

visible to be sold, the *Badis* species are anything but attractive. Don't let this fool you; the fish are hardy and once properly maintained will reward your efforts.

Since *Badis* only thrive on live foods, be sure you are able to supply them with *Tubifex*, *Daphnia*, brine shrimp or any of the usual aquarium fare. When the female becomes ripe, she is so fat that the beginning aquarist almost always assumes she has dropsy. A healthy female *Badis* is always fat; a healthy male is always slender. Color means nothing except an indication of their psychological condition.

As spawning commences, the female will enter the cave of the male where she will be subjected to some rigorous advances. Locking of lips, cichlid style, may be part of the sex play, but the usual release of eggs occurs during a

typical gourami embrace, when the male wraps his body about the female in an almost head to tail position. The embrace is not a peaceful ballet, as with gouramis, but a vigorous embrace where both fish thrash about, scattering the adhesive eggs all about the cave. The first solid object to which the eggs make contact, is the site at which they will adhere and ripen. Sometimes the male will take the eggs in his mouth and collect them into a nest, cichlid fashion, and protect and aerate them with his moving fins. At other times, he ignores them. In any case, after spawning, he drives the female out of his cave and tends the young.

The fry are seen to have ruptured their egg cases within about 2½ days, still being herded and protected by the male. As soon as the fry are free swimming, which takes another few days, they are usually safe with the male, but once they start to wander out of the cave, the male gets nervous and may eat the whole spawn. Moving the male anytime after spawning is a safe practice, but certainly remove him before the young are free swimming.

Since the young are fairly large, it would be advisable to offer them newly hatched brine shrimp as soon as they start to fend for themselves. Growth is rapid once they take brine shrimp.

The young tend to stay on the bottom of the aquarium most of the time, in small schools, and they rarely leave any brine shrimp uneaten. They grow fast and within a few weeks they are ¼ inch long with a blotchy black coloration.

The three photos on the facing page show the spawning embrace of the chameleon fish. These antics have never been reported before and the aquatic world was stunned to find a fish that acted as both a cichlid and a gourami in its spawning habits. The eggs, too tiny to be seen in the photographs, are scattered all about the inside of the flowerpot. The male will collect them and care for them. Photos by Ruda Zukal.

These might be three species of kuhli loach. The species in the rear is *Acanthophthalmus kuhlii sumatranus*; the middle fish is probably *Acanthophthalmus myersi*, while the fish in the foreground is probably a new species not yet identified. The same fishes are shown on the facing page. Photos by Vojtec Elek.

The Kuhli Loach

Acanthophthalmus semicinctus

Napoleon met his defeat in Waterloo, Belgium. I met my defeat with this fish, for every time I tried to spawn them I failed. I even went to Malaya where I caught thousands of them, but I never found any babies, nor any hint of how they spawn. The only time I ever found eggs in any adult kuhli loaches was when I received a shipment from Singapore of several thousands of them. A few very plump ones were so obviously filled with eggs (or diseased) that I

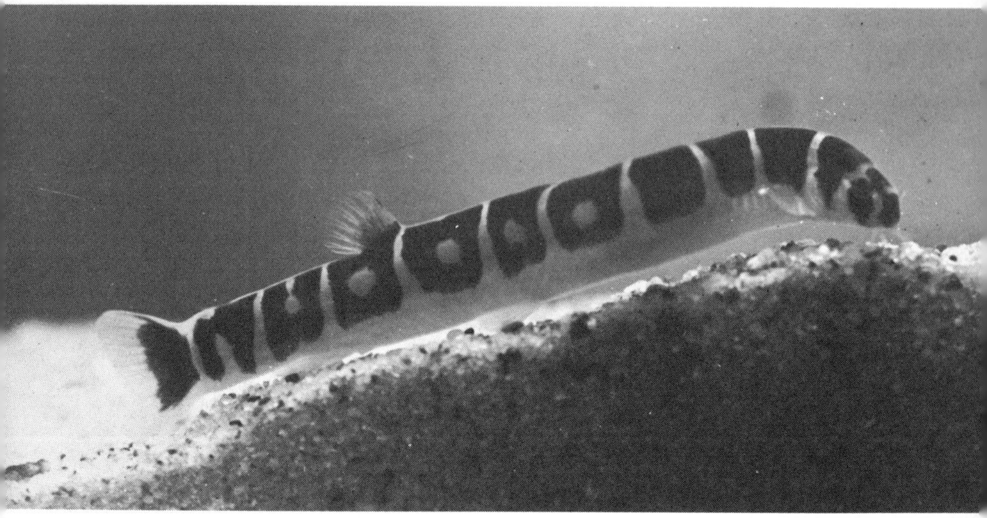

The loach above is probably a male, *A. semicinctus*, the most common species to aquarists. Photo by G. J. M. Timmerman.

sacrificed them and found them filled with bright green large eggs. Careful investigation uncovered the fact that they had benefited from a treatment of malachite green. I don't know whether or not these fish picked up the dye from the water.

The obvious question is why didn't I obtain other fat females? The answer, equally obvious, is that I couldn't find any. To catch kuhli loaches you must try during the dry season when kuhli are not in spawning condition. They hide under rocks and you collect them by simultaneously lifting a rock from their native streams and scooping under the rock with a large dipnet. You can catch quite a few this way if you are fast.

During the rainy season, when the streams are fast-moving and muddy, this method of capture is impossible since you cannot find the rocks under which they hide and they have probably moved from the rocks onto the flooded banks where they eat small insects like ants to bring themselves into spawning condition.

Above is shown another color phase of *A. semicinctus*, while the photo below is probably a female *A. myersi*. Photos by Ruda Zukal.

Above, a male *A. semicinctus*; below a female of the same species. Photos by the author.

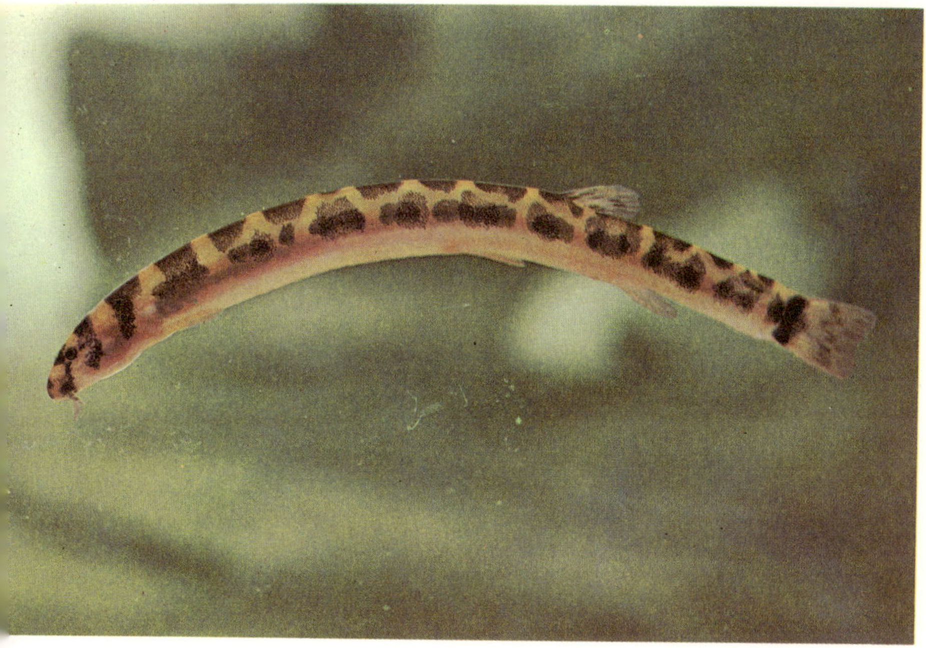

In the photos, above and below, are two varieties of *A. shelfordi*. Several experts have all of these fish belonging to the same species. Photos by the author.

Two experienced aquarists, Werner von Filek and Vojtech Elek, did report on the spawning of kuhli loaches. They wrote that it was fairly easy to spawn them. It was not easy for me! For the sake of completeness, I am quoting these articles in their entirety.

While collecting kuhli loaches all over the range in southeast Asia, I found many color varieties which, after careful examination, tended to be so close to each other in basic color pattern changes, that it must be concluded they are all the same species. Only the almost solid black kuhli loach represents a distinct species.

Von Filek's report is as follows:

During the initial courtship procedures, the male approaches the female. He comes towards her from the side, while quickly and steadily fondling her body with his whisker-studded mouth; occasionally he embraces her by pushing his body over hers in the region of the pectoral fins. The fish rarely court, and when they do, they do it in this restrained way. How long the courting lasts and whether it will finally succeed depends entirely on the bride. As long as she remains at the same spot she is not yet ready to pay attention to her swain. Only when she takes to flight does it mean that her reply is **"yes."** The surest sign for the fancier to know that his male *Acanthophthalmus* has succeeded in his courting endeavors is what we call *parallel swimming* of the partners: male and female rise from the bottom swimming side by side. The male presses his pectorals to the body of his paramour from underneath, and both swim upwards at a sharp angle while undulating harmonically. This is the upbeat for spawning! The groom wraps his caudal peduncle around the body of his bride and they release eggs and sperm simultaneously. They quickly separate, but the mating play is soon repeated again.

1

2

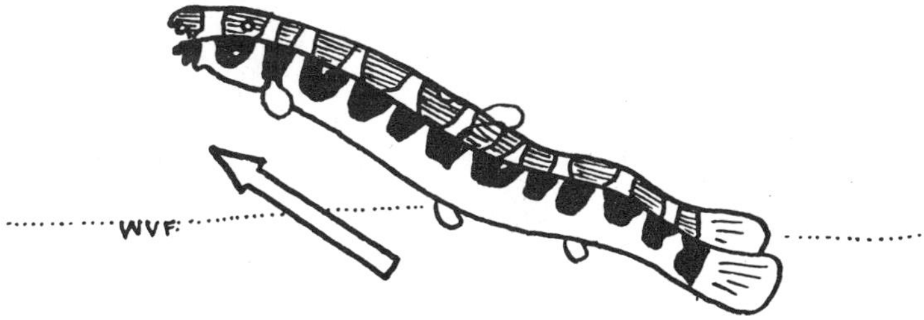

From von Filek.

3

4

Fig. 1. The shy lover cautiously approaches the chosen of his heart. She is easily identified by her thicker belly.

Fig. 2. *Acanthophthalmus semicinctus* "embraces" his bride. She does nothing to show that she accepts her ardent lover.

Fig. 3. Readiness for spawning. As soon as the female runs away, Mr. Kuhli knows that his wooing has been accepted. Nestling closely together, the pair swim upwards and pitch each other into ever-increasing excitement.

Fig. 4. "He" embraces "her" with his tail and they release eggs and sperm nearly simultaneously. Then both sink to the bottom, exhausted, and rest for a while after which the mating game starts all over again.

All four fish shown on these facing pages are color varieties of *Acanthophthalmus shelfordi*. One authority says they are all *semicinctus*. Having checked thousands of fish with this color pattern, I have never found a heavy female. Photos by the author.

How do the pairs recognize each other? The fancier who keeps kuhli loaches in his tank will notice which of the fish is the female by her thickened belly. But will the same feature also help the male *Acanthophthalmus*? It seems as if this is not the case. The peculiar manner of courting, which is much more pronounced and differentiated from that of other loaches, leads to the conclusion that the sense of smell plays a quite more important part.

Numerous experiments with the European gudgeon, *Noemacheilus barbatulus*, have confirmed this supposition, for both dummies and other males were approached and touched in the same manner as females by rutting fellow males. This makes optical recognition unlikely. On the other hand it is a known fact that fishes have odors that are specific for each species and that loaches have sensory organs for the reception of chemical stimuli. Why, then, should no specific sexual odors be present? Add to this that most loaches come from muddy waters where optical means of recognition lose their meaning. The disturbance during courting muddies the water further still, and visual conditions become even worse.

There are many open questions about the genus *Acanthophthalmus*, and the observation of fanciers are especially important if we want to close all gaps in our knowledge about these interesting fishes.

Vojtech Elek's report is as follows:

"Are these things fish, too?" is the general query of the curious visitor when he discovers some kuhli loaches in your tank. The question does not lack a certain reason, for these loaches look like striped worms rather than ornamental fish. The non-aquarist needs some imagination if he is to identify these wormlike animals as fishes. At the most he will consider the snakelike kuhli loaches as being little eels.

My first experience with these interesting fishes of the family Cobitidae occurred about five years ago, when on a whim I picked up a dozen or so. I brought them home and put them into a small all-glass tank, intending to transfer them to larger quarters eventually. When I finally got around to trying to make the transfer, it seemed that the fish were going to thwart me, because they made it very difficult for me to catch them. They flitted and rushed around the tank so quickly that it looked to me as if there were five times more of them than I knew were actually in the tank. If by chance one of them entered the net, it immediately reversed itself and got out again. The whole operation made me highly respectful of the fish-catching abilities of the shopowner from whom I bought the fish. He had caught them easily enough; I couldn't. In frustration I gave the whole operation with the net up as a bad job and simply upended the tank, catching the loaches in a net as the water poured out.

They retired as soon as they were quartered in their new home. In order to afford them hiding places, I had placed three small plastic tubes into the tank, and they immediately withdrew into them, even though the tank was well-stocked with plants. To make the loaches' sojourn especially nice, I had added shredded fibers of peat moss to the bottom covering, so that it became slightly mulmy. For a few weeks nothing happened and it seemed as if I had an empty tank standing in my home. Later on the loaches still squeezed into the plastic tubes during daylight, and left their housing hesitantly only when dusk fell, sliding along the bottom and foraging for food. Their manner of swimming had something of the gliding of a snake. Suddenly, as if wanting to make up for lost time, they shot lightninglike along the viewing pane, made a fast turnabout a fraction of an inch before its end, and rushed back. After a short time the frolic finished; as if on command the fish slid slowly back to the bottom, and within a few minutes the play was repeated

In handling more than 250,000 kuhli loaches, I have always found heavy, fat female *semicinctus* like that in the lower photo, but I have never found a female with the coloration shown in the upper photo. Photos by the author.

again. Only at dawn did they glide back into their tubes again. That is, they slid into *one* of the tubes, for only very rarely would a single fish lose its way into an empty one. I surmised that kuhli loaches love company, even if things get a little crowded.

The size, shape of the head and position of the barbels almost surely verifies the difference in species; coloration does not seem to be important with the genus *Acanthophthalmus*. Photo by Vojtec Elek.

Months passed without my seeing anything of the fish. But since I had to care for several tanks anyway, the loach tank too received its share automatically. The plants had already grown into a dense jungle, so that my view through the tank became increasingly obstructed, but despite this I never showed the courage to look deeper into things, fearing that the loaches might have disappeared.

But they were still there, and one evening I was able to witness a very exciting event. When I entered my fish room, moonlight was playing over their tank, and what I saw is hard to describe. The fish are normally swift swimmers, but what took place in front of my eyes now was a real rodeo. I really *sensed* the excitement that prevailed in the tank. The loaches shot through the tank in pairs, whirled around their longitudinal axes, and showed a coloration I could hardly have imagined. I recognized the three females very easily, for they were full and rounded in the belly part, and looked "inflated" in comparison to the males. Sexing fish that are not ripe for spawning is very difficult. Cautious hobbyists buy several specimens in the hope that "at least two of them have to be a pair."

I checked the tank again at about the same time the following night, hoping to see a repetition of the action, but everything was quiet. There were no longer any obviously egg-laden fish in the tank, however, so I concluded that the spawning had taken place. I looked eagerly for eggs or fry but was able to find nothing. And nothing more of interest happened in the loach tank until the following spring, at which time the fish that I assumed to be the females again filled up with eggs.

This time I was going to know things in detail: I set up a larger all-glass tank, put in fine-grained sand, mixed with a little peat moss, poured in some rain water, and kept the level low—ideal conditions, in my opinion. I had also doped out a new method of transferring the fish: the little plastic tube in which my loaches dwelt was closed with leaves at

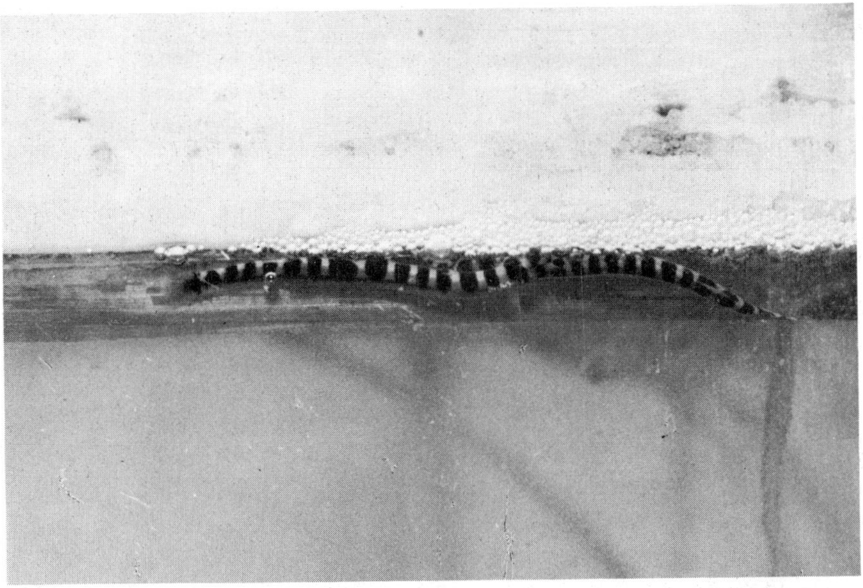

After my kuhli loaches went through this embrace under a bubblenest, babies appeared several weeks later. Are they spawning here? They were the only two fish in the aquarium. Photos by the author.

both ends and thus transferred to the breeding tank. Unfortunately, they did not like their new home at all, and after a few days I moved them back to their old tank. The very next night the turbulent mating dance witnessed the year before started all over again. The fish rushed and flitted excitedly around the tank, showing their gorgeous colors once more. On the third evening the uproar was over and the fish disappeared as if they had vanished from earth. When I saw them again some time later, the females looked as slender as if they had gone to a reducing spa.

According to what I have seen and noticed over the five-year period in which I have kept various "kuhli loach" species (I have three distinct species), the females get ready for spawning only once a year. Whether this is true in their native waters, I don't know; perhaps someone who regularly breeds kuhli loaches and successfully raises the fry will throw some light on the subject for us.

The Scissorstail Rasbora

Rasbora trilineata

BY DR. HERBERT R. AXELROD

For many years every fish in the genus *Rasbora* was considered as a very difficult fish to breed and keep alive! The basis for these judgments was the terrible experience everyone had with "the" *Rasbora*, meaning the most popular of all rasboras, *Rasbora heteromorpha*. In the old days, before 1954, *Rasbora heteromorpha* were collected by the millions in the streams outside Singapore, brought into the city and stored in huge glass bowls until one of the four or five fish buyers arrived. In 1952 I made the trip to Singapore, com-

These three photos show the sex differences between the fat female scissorstail rasbora and the male. Lower photo by Dr. Stanislav Frank; other photos by Ruda Zukal.

The scissorstail changes pigment intensity with the background. These three photographs show clearly the basic color pattern and the difference between plump, ripe females and active males. When females are this heavy, spawning is guaranteed. Photos by Ruda Zukal.

peting with Auguste Rabaut for the purchase of 250,000 *Rasbora heteromorpha*. I was able to buy them all for US $2,000, which is less than 1¢ each! I then put them into plastic lined wooden boxes on board a ship and cared for them hourly on the two month journey to America. By the time I reached Staten Island, New York I had lost about 100,000 of the 250,000. Within the next ten days, as their water was changed and changed, more were lost until, I estimate, probably 50,000 of the original 250,000 reached petshops. At that time I sold them for 75¢ each as the basic wholesale price. Of course, I had the chance to bring in many other fishes at the same time since my cost of the air conditioned, heated room on the boat was the same regardless of how much I put into it.

Spawning sequences shown in these four photos by Ruda Zukal, show the male trying to lead the female into the spawning grass where they will spray their tiny eggs. Photos by Ruda Zukal.

While collecting *Rasbora heteromorpha*, many other species are caught as well, and when the collectors separated the various species from the "money fish," a few odds and ends always escaped their quick eyes. On this particular trip in 1952 I ended up with a few hundred scissorstail rasbora, *Rasbora trilineata*. What impressed me most about this fish is that none died on the whole trip!

After selling most of the fishes I brought from Singapore, I was left with the same few hundred scissorstails; nobody who saw them wanted them. I had to sell them to someone who didn't know what they looked like, for their drab appearance certainly didn't help their cause when compared to *heteromorpha*.

When the boat docked in New York with the fishes, I usually rented an empty store and set up shop for a week until I sold everything I had. When I was left with anything, I would call up some of the larger dealers and offer them special prices. There were no takers at any price for the scissorstails. So, just as I was about to throw them into formalin and allow some of my students to study them at New York University, I received a telephone call from a friend in Florida, a fish farmer, who wanted to know if I had any "oddballs worth breeding." I almost said "No," when I saw the only fish left in the store . . . *scissorstails*. "Would you like a new *Rasbora*?" "Sure would," came the reply, "how much are they?" The deal was made and when my friend in Florida saw the fish he refused to pay me for them, and at that time I couldn't blame him.

About a year later the market was flooded with *Rasbora trilineata*. My "friend" in Florida successfully bred them and they became very popular because they were so graceful, hardy and peaceful. Just the right kind of fish to go with a peaceful community aquarium.

Even to this day, the scissorstail rasbora is the only *Rasbora* species bred in any quantity in Florida . . . or any place in the world, for that matter.

A side view and head-on view of the spawning pair. Photos by Ruda Zukal.

The scissorstail rasbora is probably the most-spawned-by-aquarists rasbora. It is simple to spawn the fish if you have a pair which are easily sexed. These three photos show the fish spawning in *Fontinalis*, a cold-water plant. Photos by Ruda Zukal.

You, too, can easily breed this hardy, peaceful fish. The spawning tank should be small, not larger than ten gallons, planted heavily with bushy plants or artificial spawning grass. The water should be in the high 70's, slightly acid with a pH of 6.2 to 6.9, and as soft as possible. Artificially softened water is the best as that is what is used in Florida where the water is naturally hard and very alkaline. The breeders, which should be about two inches long or larger, should be easily sexed. The male is very slender both from a top view and a front view, when compared with a bulging fat female. Two males for each female is advised.

The males will chase the female into the thickets, one at a time usually, rubbing against her in a parallel head-to-head position, expelling about 20 eggs at each spawning attempt. Several hundred eggs are laid. If the breeders

As the male leads the female into the plants, he rubs against her in a side-by-side position and they scatter eggs amongst the vegetation. These three photos were taken seconds apart by Ruda Zukal.

have been well fed (they eat everything), they usually won't eat their own spawn.

I usually raise the temperature of the water to about 85° to induce spawning, but this isn't necessary as many of my colleagues spawn the fish equally well without any temperature adjustments. At 85°, however, the eggs hatch in less than 24 hours, so be prepared to remove the parents the first evening whether they have completed spawning or not.

The fry do best on infusoria for a week before they are offered newly hatched brine shrimp. If only brine shrimp is available, then about 40% of the fry will be lost as there will be many which are too small to eat this relatively large food. In all cases offer your newly hatched fry only the San Francisco variety of newly hatched brine shrimp, as the Utah shrimp are too large for most newly hatched egg-laying fishes.

The white tips on the ventral fins of the upper fish distinguish it as a male. Photo by Ruda Zukal.

A pair of pencilfish, in a quiet community aquarium, lends subtle variation and interest to the aquarium hobby. The pencilfish never attacks anything that it cannot eat in its tiny mouth!

The Pencilfish

Poecilobrycon eques

In the many years that I have fished hundreds, if not thousands of streams throughout Brazil, I can always tell beforehand if I am going to find these beautiful little pencilfish. They always seem to prefer shaded, clear water which moves very slowly and which has a very dense vegetation. They are never found in large rivers, deep pools or stagnant shallow water. They are never visible when I inspect a stream, but they show up later after we have thoroughly seined the area, pushing our steel-rimmed nets into the vegetation to get the rare fish which bury in the soft mulm and hide amongst the drooping leaves.

In these four photographs by Ruda Zukal, a female pencilfish searches for the underside of a leaf upon which to deposit her spawn. When a male sees this action, he actively pursues her, waiting for the laying of eggs which he can fertilize.

Even though this fish is plump, don't be fooled. This is a male that has just enjoyed a meal of newly hatched brine shrimp. Males have the white tips to their ventral fins. Photo by Ruda Zukal.

A perfect pair of pencilfish. The plump female in front of the active male. Photo by Ruda Zukal.

This pencilfish, sometimes referred to as the "slant swimmer" because of its constant 45° tail-down pose, is a fish for the more idealistic hobbyist. This fish has quiet beauty and dignity; only the red anal fin has any colorful significance, but it is one of my favorite fish. Try what I did for such a long time. Put a few glass goldfish bowls (with undergravel filters and heaters, of course) in some obscure corner of the house. Put the slender males, whose colors seem more intense than the females in one bowl and the females in the other. They thrive on freshly hatched brine shrimp and fine floating foods. Only use freeze-dried foods as they float for hours. Any food which sinks is completely ignored and will only foul the small bowl.

Having found a spawning site, the male aligns his body with that of the female under a sturdy leaf, and the pair, in this series of three photos, deposit their spawn on the underside of the leaf. Photos by Ruda Zukal.

As soon as the females fatten up prepare the tank for the spawning. I use *Cryptocoryne* plants for pencilfish seem to like to hide and spawn amongst the sturdy leaves of these plants. Plant one or two *Cryptocoryne* plants in the bowls and take a few of the males and put them in with the females, while at the same time you have put some females in with the males. The water temperature should be raised significantly, from 75° for maintaining the fish to 85 or 90° for spawning. Soft, slightly acid (pH6.5 to 6.8), clear water is essential.

As soon as the commotion of the move settles down, the males will discover the females and slowly, *very slowly*, pursue them. While the males were kept together they completely ignored one another, but as soon as both of them spy a female, they become enemies and while they rarely attack each other, they are anything but friendly. The female seems disinterested in which male follows her, but as soon as she acknowledges that at least one male is interested, she begins to inspect the underside of a leaf. This inspection can last for a few minutes or a few hours, but finally a male

A family of pencilfish. Photo by N.Y. Zoological Society.

A bottom view of a pair of pencilfish. The female's obvious swollen abdomen is caused by eggs which she is most anxious to place underneath broad-leafed plants. The attentive male will follow her and fertilize the eggs as they are laid. Photo by Ruda Zukal.

swims to her side under the leaf she has chosen and together they spawn. The male fertilizes the adhesive eggs as soon as the female deposits them on the underside of the leaf. At times a few of the tiny eggs fall to the bottom of the tank where they are ignored.

Remove the breeders after spawning and calculate on 50–100 eggs for each female. If possible the males should outnumber the females two to one.

The eggs hatch in less than 48 hours and the fry require infusoria for several weeks until they are large enough to take newly hatched brine shrimp. Raising the fry is much more difficult than getting the breeders to spawn.

Probably the first pair of lionhead cichlids to come out of Africa alive were these collected by the author in the Stanley Pool in 1958. The male, upper fish, has a more obvious fleshy protuberance on his forehead than the female, lower fish. Photo by the author.

The Lionhead Cichlid

Steatocranus casuarius

It was very late at night and Pierre Brichard, the famous fish collector, and his daughter, Mirielle, had just introduced me to night-fishing in the Stanley Pool outside of Kinshasa, Congo. I suppose we caught 2,000 *Synodontis nigriventris*, the upsidedown catfish, within an hour as they were everywhere visible in the lights we were wearing on our heads. Of course it took many more hours to extricate them from the net as their spines had to be delicately removed from the nylon mesh without damaging either fish or net. While all this activity was going on I went back to the rocky part of the pool to sit down and rest. Almost at my feet was an old rubber boot and when I lifted it out of the water I realized there was a pair of fish in the boot. I later discovered that pair had a nest and they were lionhead cichlids, *Steatocranus casuarius*.

It was a simple matter to get more of these interesting fish and we found many of them. The older the fish, the larger the lump; both males and females shared this fleshy protuberance.

The lionhead cichlid is one of those cichlids whose ventral fins enable it to sit, at an angle, on the bottom of the aquarium in a fashion similar to the oscar (*Astronotus*). This head-on view shows the dome-like forehead of a male. Photo by Peter Chlupaty.

The lionhead cichlid is one of the most available of the African cichlids, probably because it is found in Brichard's immediate collecting area and it is so hardy. For an African cichlid, this is a very peaceful fish and you don't have to worry about them fighting amongst themselves if you supply them with flowerpots in which they can hide and spawn.

A young pair of breeders. As soon as the male develops the fleshy protuberance on his head, he is usually mature enough to spawn. The female spawns at this same size though she hasn't developed a fleshy protuberance.

To breed the lionhead, all you need is a well-fed pair and a large flowerpot in which the fish can have privacy and a feeling of security. The male is seen emerging from the flowerpot. Spawning is very private and any light inhibits spawning activity.

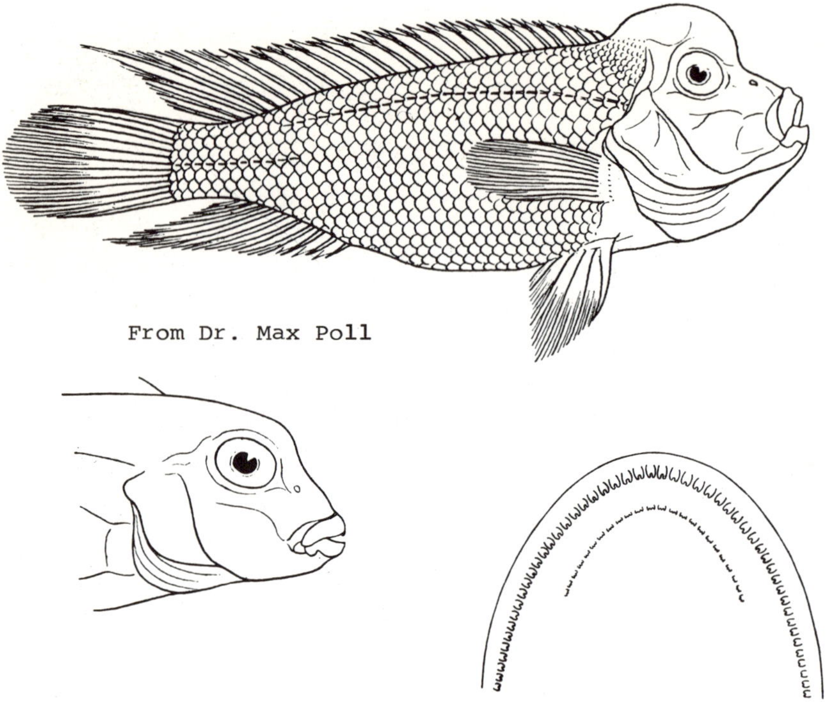

Scientists use illustrations like these to show the lionhead cichlid, the shape of the female's head and the position of the teeth. I feel the drawing is incorrect in that the caudal peduncle is too narrow.

Spawning is a very private affair and all attempts at photographing it have, thus far, been in vain. If you tilt the flowerpot so you can see into it, the pair either leave the pot or spit gravel into the opening to seal it. I have, however, developed the following method of spawning these fish.

Set up as large an aquarium as possible. Plant it well and locate enough flowerpots to accommodate every pair of fish. Try to get a dozen small lionhead cichlids and let them grow up and pair off by natural selection. The female, immediately prior to spawning will enter the flowerpot of the male of her choice and lay her eggs. Before she does this there is a lot of earth-moving and the pair rearrange the

Compare this photograph of a female with the body shape of the outline on the facing page. Quite different, isn't it? Photo by Gerhard Marcuse.

gravel to suit their own purposes. Once the gravel moving ceases, the pair usually begin spawning by laying about 100 eggs on the inside roof of the flowerpot. Both parents dutifully guard and assumedly aerate the eggs and care for the young until they fend for themselves. I have often seen the male and female separately take mouthfuls of food and spit it into the nest, bringing food to their fry. Commercially, I usually remove the flowerpot with the eggs and substitute an airstone for the parents. The fry can take newly hatched brine shrimp as soon as they leave the flowerpot.

The breeders are not sensitive to water types, but I use soft, slightly acid water (pH6.8, DH 6). I feed the breeders live *Tubifex* worms and freeze-dried brine shrimp. Freeze-dried flake foods are also greedily taken when the fish are hungry.

It is very possible to raise several families in the same tank without removing any of the breeders or the fry, but it is not recommended if you are making a living breeding fish!

The young pair brought back from the Stanley Pool by the author. The male, upper fish, is probably less than one year old, but as he gets older, his fleshy protuberance becomes quite exaggerated, as can be seen in the male illustrated below.

A pair of gold barbs from Czechoslovakia. This photograph was taken by Dr. Stanislav Frank in Prague and shows a male (fish to the left) and female.

The Albino Schuberti

Capoeta species

Fortunately, this is not a book concerning itself with the problems of taxonomy. The correct identification of these fish would be impossible. They do not exist in Nature and even the supposedly wild form from which they came has never been verified. I have chosen the scientific name *Capoeta* because the fish was supposed to have evolved from *Capoeta semifasciolatus* when a few golden sports showed up in the aquariums of the late Tom Schubert of Camden, New Jersey. Later, during the late 1960's a pure golden variety appeared in Czechoslovakia as evidenced by a photograph sent to me by Dr. Stanislav Frank of Prague. This golden sport had black eyes. Then, in 1970, Denis Wilcox of Lakeland, Florida sent me a few pairs of true albino barbs. All of these sports, as well as the supposed original stock, are illustrated with color photographs.

To breed these fish requires little skill. Separate the males from the females and feed them heavily for a few weeks until the females are very plump and the males have developed small white pimples on their faces. Oftentimes these pimples (nuptial tubercles) are missing and the male spawns anyway, but use two males to each female if the males do not show these pimples.

Denis Wilcox of V–W Fish Hatcheries in Lakeland, Florida, found the first albino gold barbs in his hatchery aquariums.

Early in 1960, Ruda Zukal found gold barbs which had almost no markings. From these barbs came the gold barb with black eyes. Photo by Ruda Zukal.

Conditioning the fish is the most important part of the job. Barbs, especially albino and golden barbs, will eat anything. They are so gluttonous that they gobble down dry food before it has soaked up its full measure of water, and the food often swells in their stomachs causing them to bloat and have difficulty swimming for an hour or so. This doesn't seem to be serious. Live foods and freeze-dried foods suit them perfectly and in a month the females will be full of roe.

The spawning tank should be as large as possible with a trio of fish, two males and one female. The tank should have spawning grass covering the bottom and one side so the breeders can dash into the thickets and, rubbing against each other side by side, scatter their almost non-adhesive eggs wherever they may fall. If the breeders are not well fed they might gobble up their spawn as quickly as they lay the eggs, so observe them carefully.

Denis Wilcox's albino barb in the photo above is identical in almost all physical measurements to the "normal" golden barbs shown in the photo on the facing page, except for its lack of color and the red eyes. Albinos photographed by the author; golden barbs photographed by Dr. K. Knaack.

The photograph above and on the facing page have very historic value. These are the first photographs of the almost colorless barbs which were called "Barbus schuberti" after Tom Schubert of Camden, New Jersey who was supposed to have "discovered" them. No one has ever found barbs with this kind of marking in nature any place in the world, so their "discovery" was probably a distortion of the truth and the fish is not entitled to a scientific name. Tank-bred variations carry the same scientific name as the original stock even though they barely have resemblance, thus a great dane dog and a chihuahua are scientifically known by the same name.

If you want albino fish it would be best to breed albino males with albino females. Often albinos are difficult fish to spawn so I have successfully used normal golden fish (either males or females) as one of the partners, and then used their offspring for breeding stock. This gave me about 25% albino offspring, the balance being golden with black eyes. This 25% albino usually ended being more albinos than I would get from breeding albino to albino. The usual pure albino spawn would be about 60 fry; the golden **X** albino would produce 500 fry and more than 100 albinos would be my normal expectation.

The fry are free of their egg shells in less than two days and are free swimming in about six days after which they require copious amounts of infusoria for a few days and then freshly hatched brine shrimp. Water temperature should be over 80° and the water must be clean. The pH is not too important, nor is the hardness but pH6.8 with 14 DH suits them well.

A closeup of a pair of albino barbs sent to the author by Denis Wilcox, the first man to discover them among a spawn of gold barbs. Albino barbs do not exist as a separate race in the wild. Photo by the author.

The original pair of emperor tetras from which almost all the tank-raised fish originated. These fish were collected by the author and given to Dr. Eduard Schmidt-Focke in Germany, who was probably the first man to breed them. Photo by the author.

The Emperor Tetra

Nematobrycon palmeri

On an expedition I made to Colombia in 1959, I was very lucky to rediscover two species of *Nematobrycon* which had never been seen alive by aquarists. The Pacific side of the Andes is not very rich in colorful species when compared to the Amazon side, but there are certain beautiful fishes which should be brought in for aquarists to breed. The two *Nematobrycon* seemed to me to be excellent species, but only *palmeri* was bred and is now firmly established in the aquatic trade. Both species, *palmeri* and *amphiloxus*, share

A mature male, in the photo above, has longer fins and is larger than the female (lower photo) of the same species. Neither fish is in spawning condition, thus their light coloration. Photo by Ruda Zukal.

In a light colored environment, the fish are pale, while the same fish become much darker and more colorful as their aquarium is darkened in the photograph below. Photos by Ruda Zukal.

In a darkened spawning tank, the male (upper photograph) attempts to push the female into the plant thickets. On the facing page, the two photographs show the blue-eyed male trying to force the female into a clump of *Fontinalis*, but she evades him and, in the lower photo on the facing page, the pair circle each other spraying eggs.

Photos by Hans Joachim Richter.

with certain African characins, the extension of the middle rays of their caudal fins and they have very similar habits even though they are found thousands of miles from each other. The Congo tetra, *Phenacogrammus interruptus* has, as its chief physical attribute, a longer and more delicate caudal extension, but the emperor tetra is easier to breed and much more colorful in body.

The habitat of the fish in the Rio Atrato area where I found it, is in very clean, soft, slightly acid water. The small streams are filled with bushy plants in which the parents spawn and the fry thrive. In the aquarium breeding them is simple.

Select about a dozen fish to begin with. Keep them in pure water to which no chemicals have been added. I have found that rain water which has been aged for several months in the dark is an ideal spawning solution. The pH of such water is usually less than 6.0 and it doesn't matter if it is as low as 4.8 since the fish thrive in it. Keep the males and females separate. I made the mistake initially of keeping the males in adjacent tanks to the females only to watch the females spawn just by being excited from the fluttering males in an adjacent tank.

The Congo tetra, *Phenacogrammus interruptus* is another fish which has the same caudal extension as the emperor tetra. In both species the male's tail has a longer and more vivid elongation than the female's. Photo by Timmerman.

After feeding the fishes well on live and freeze-dried foods for a month, I set up bare tanks which are almost completely covered with spawning grasses. Artificial spawning grass serves as well as the usual fine-leaved natural plants like *Myriophyllum* and *Elodea*. When I find a very active male and a very full female, I put them into a small aquarium of about $2\frac{1}{2}$ gallons capacity and fill it with unused rain water and the spawning grass. I introduce the pair of fish immediately before sunset, giving the fish the whole night to become acclimated to the new surroundings. The fish almost always spawn within the next 48 hours. The majority of them spawn the second morning. Spawns are small, about 100 eggs, and the breeders go through the usual characin spawning effort, with mad dashes into the thickets, scattering eggs as they go. Once the fish begin to spawn, they are rarely hindered by flashbulbs or prying eyes and they continue for hours. I have timed spawnings that took as long as five hours before they were finished. The usual spawning times are from 8:00 AM to 1:00 PM on the second day of their introduction to the spawning tank. The breeders should be removed the evening of the second day, whether they've spawned or not. The eggs hatch, in water of 78°F., in 30 hours and the fry are very tiny and very sensitive.

Many males seem to be sterile. Out of 27 spawnings I have documented, I found 14 males were unable to fertilize the eggs even though they went through the motions. I verified this by switching pairs around, using the same females with other males and vice versa. I have not discovered the cause of this sterility nor any visual signs which differentiate a functional male from a sterile one, but if you keep accurate spawning records you will find the good males and, of course, you should dispose of the non-functional specimens. I have never found any females which were barren.

The fry require copious amounts of infusoria and when you get the right food for them, you'll have remarkable

A magnificent pair of emperor tetras, with the male below the female. Photo by Hans Joachim Richter.

The pair spawning onto the fine leaves of a *Myriophyllum scabratum* strand. Photo by Hans Joachim Richter.

success. I remove the spawning medium carefully as soon as the young have become free swimming. This gives the young a better chance at catching the infusoria. This also points out the need for the small tank. By leaving a light on in one corner of the aquarium you will find both the fry and the phototropic infusoria congregating by the light and growth is faster. After two weeks the fry are able to take newly hatched San Francisco brand brine shrimp (the Utah brand is too large for their small mouths at this early

As the female gets older, she is no longer able to spawn and she slows down considerably, keeping her fins folded most of the time. Photo by Gerhard Marcuse.

A young pair of breeding conditioned emperor tetras. The larger of the fish is the male, above, sporting a beautiful tail. The lower fish is a female, ripe with eggs. The plant is *Cyperus alternifolius*.

age, but is suitable for later feedings.) Several batches of fry have died from what might have been too much DDT in the brine shrimp eggs. A report I read on the comparison of the DDT content of these eggs shows that Utah eggs have about four times as much DDT in them as California eggs, so keep this in mind should you have a problem with raising fry on newly hatched brine shrimp.

After the young are free swimming, raise the temperature to about 82°F. for more rapid growth, but always be sure the fish are feeding on the almost invisible infusoria. If their little bellies are not rounded, you better look at the culture carefully under a microscope to be sure there is live food in the culture.

Always keep your emperor tetras sexually separated. They are magnificent fish for any community aquarium and they do especially well if kept with no other species.

A very young pair of *Epiplatys chaperi*, previous known as *E. sheljuzkoi*. The very young male, the upper fish, has more dots covering his body than the female below him. Photo by the author.

Sheljuzhkoi

Epiplatys chaperi

The recent works of Col. Jorgen Scheel have resulted in the changing of much of the killifish nomenclature and, unfortunately, this fish is one of those which has had its name changed. It was previously known as *Epiplatys sheljuzhkoi*. In Book I of this series of *Breeding Aquarium Fishes* I have shown another fish with the same name. If you compare the fins and color pattern of the males you can readily see that they are not the same fish, however.

Epiplatys are very easy to care for and even easier to spawn. Use as small an aquarium as possible. I use one gallon plastic filter boxes, the kind that hang outside the aquarium for the larger power filters. I set up a dozen or so, using floating spawning mops (these are just strands of nylon used for knitting, tied at the top, with their severed ends hanging loosely in the water). The fish merely swim into the nylon and drop a few eggs every time they spawn. Spawning takes place for weeks with about ten eggs a day being produced. I remove the nylon material every week and hatch all the spawns at the same time.

The eggs take about ten days to hatch and I have found the best way to raise them is in shallow, white enamel trays. As the young appear I net them out and raise them separately from the next day's hatch since a day or two is enough difference in size for brother to eat brother. The fry are large enough to greedily gobble newly hatched brine shrimp and they thrive on that diet.

If you spawn your fish in a regular aquarium, you will have quite a problem collecting the eggs for they spawn on anything that has a frilly appearance. I have had them spawn

A magnificent male photographed by Jørgen Scheel, from his book *Rivulins of the Old World*.

A mature male, in the photo above; below a mature female. The body, dorsal fin and tail of the male are more dotted than the female's. Photos by Ruda Zukal.

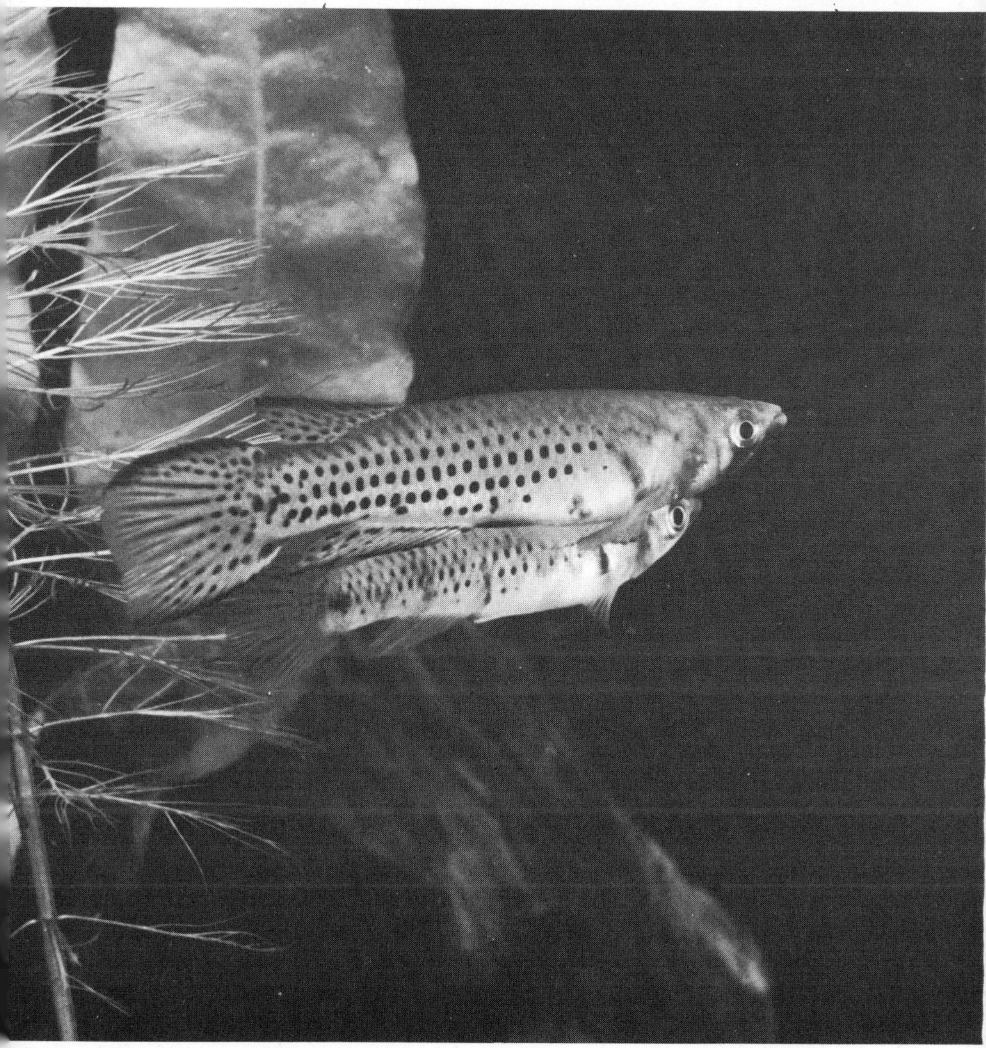

As the pair develop a spawning interest, the male begins to crowd the female more and more, forcing her to lay eggs in almost every plant in the aquarium. Photos by Ruda Zukal.

Closeup details of the pair as they begin spawning. In the upper photo the pair are spawning near the top of the tank, while in the lower photo the pair are spawning in *Fontinalis* on the bottom. Photos by Ruda Zukal.

Front, head-on view (above) and side view (below) of a spawning pair. The fish align themselves almost perfectly when spawning. Photos by Ruda Zukal.

These three photographs show the beginning of spawning, the same fish two weeks later, and the same fish one month after being together, with the female completely depleted of eggs (above). Photos by Ruda Zukal.

on exposed plant roots, Spanish moss, *Elodea*, *Myriophyllum* and once they even spawned on an old net that had fallen into the water! Several breeders say that they never spawn in the same place twice if they have a chance. Perhaps this is so. I maintain the fish in soft, acid water at 74°.

To condition the breeders they must be separated and placed in relative isolation. Feed the fish heavily prior to spawning. They thrive on ants and wingless fruit flies if you are able to provide these. Live brine shrimp and *Tubifex* are satisfactory substitutes . . . but they are only substitutes. (You should try your hand at breeding fruit flies. See Col. Jorgen Scheel's book *Rivulins of the Old World* for more complete information.) After the females have been fattened up for a month, put them together with the males. Use two males to each female if possible and allow the fish to remain together for about one month, then separate them for one month, and start all over again. The fish must be fed while they are spawning or they might eat their own eggs. Egg cannabalism is not usual with this species.

The young grow quickly and usually can spawn in three to six months depending upon how well they are fed and maintained.

A young pair of spotted headstanders. Photo by G. J. M. Timmerman.

The Spotted Headstander

Chilodus punctatus

This is a very difficult fish to breed and I have never successfully spawned the spotted headstander, although I have captured many of them in Brazil. One of my close friends, and one of the world's most capable aquarists, is Hans Joachim Franke. He lives in Gera, East Germany and he concentrates on the more difficult fish. He spawned the spotted headstander about a dozen times and I tried everything he recommended but I couldn't duplicate his feat. I always used imported fish, while Franke used fish already tank-bred; this makes quite a difference. Rather than give a synopsis of Franke's experience, I have his permission to reproduce his notes as he offered them to me and which I translated as follows:

As far back as March, 1959, I became acquainted with Chilodus punctatus *and have since had opportunities to observe and to photograph their spawning. From nine spawnings I have raised about a thousand youngsters. Before giving a detailed account of this I would like to make a few general observations.*

This fish belongs to the family Anostomidae, the small-mouthed characins, to which modern taxonomy has assigned a separate family. According to Professor Sterba, the following nine genera come under this heading: Abramites, Anostomus, Chilodus, Curimatopsis, Curimatus, Laemolyta, Leporinus, Prochilodus, *and* Tylobranchus.

All of these genera inhabit the lower reaches of the water, where they prefer to search the bottom for nourishment. Not being the best of swimmers, they prefer to seek the protection afforded by reedy areas. Probably their tilted head-down position can be assumed to be an adaptation to their unique way of life, because when they are among the reed-stalks they can scarcely be distinguished by the predators. This swimming position is not confined only to mature specimens; in their first days of life the young assume an even more vertical position.

The family Anostomidae is native to northern and central South America, southern Central America and also the West Indies. Here they are found in slowly flowing or standing waters in small schools. In spite of the fact that some

A young, wild headstander which has a disease manifested by the shiny metallic deposit under the scales above the lateral line to the rear of the eye. Photo by Harald Schultz.

of them get to be 16 inches long they can be kept in the community aquarium because they are completely peaceful. The torpedo-shaped body ends in front with a very pointed head. The tiny mouth has only a few teeth and is not adapted to catching the larger foods. Because they have large bodies to nourish they are forced to be constantly hunting for food, which in their native waters would probably consist mostly of tubifex worms and Chironomus *larvae.*

The fish seem to be comfortable at temperatures between 77 and 81°, although temperatures as low as 68° are endured without ill effects.

In addition, the total carbon dioxide content often went to 19.5, when the water came fresh from the tap. Comparing both analyses, it became clear that C. punctatus *is very insensitive to water hardness and ionic content of the water.*

Sex differences can be distinguished with certainty only when spawning time is at hand. Then the bellies of the females are considerably deeper. Color differences are very slight, and sexes cannot be distinguished in this way without a great deal of difficulty at other times.

All in all the spotted headstanders are good aquarium fish which frequently reach the astounding age for Anostomids of 5 years and more.

In February 1962 the Chilodus *females began to show slight signs that their eggs were ripening, and at the same time the males began driving. When two males met they immediately assumed threatening poses, where they placed their bodies together and spread their fins (to trigger this behavior certain impulses are necessary which release the specific reactions. This might be, for instance, a sudden color change in the opponents, certain fin movements, or many other things.) The males would make beating motions against each other with their bodies. All this took place in their typically slanted position, but suddenly they began to describe circles, where one tried to bite the other near the tail. When doing this, they assumed a horizontal position. Van den Nieuwenhuizen observed and photographed a similar procedure with* Anostomus taeniatus, *which shows a closely related ethological relationship to the* Chilodus *and* Leporinus *species. These battles always end in the same manner, with one or the other quickly seeking refuge in the plants. The victor generally follows, but the defeated fish is left alone as soon as he assumes the pose which indicates that he has had enough.*

When males meet females they immediately attempt to attract attention, but the latter take no notice and swim away hurriedly. Frequently the male follows, bumping her ventral region with his mouth and pushing her ahead of him in this manner.

The ventral region of both females became more rounded and one morning I saw a pair going through mating motions in a clump of Nomaphila stricta. *I decided that the time for spawning attempts had come.*

Based on the experience of Dr. Geisler, I set up a spawning aquarium (20 × 20 × 12 inches) bare of gravel but with a pillow of Java moss,

Vesicularia dubyana *and a bundle of* Nomaphila stricta, *the latter with leaves that reached to the water's surface. The very soft aged water measured 2.3 DH and had a pH value of 6.8. In this I put the pair which had gone through the false mating.*

A few hours later the male began driving furiously. At first he assumed the attention-getting pose, taking a position alongside the female with outspread fins and at the same time making beating motions with his body. As the female was still not adequately stimulated, the male began to bite her repeatedly in the ventral region. As a result, the female took refuge in a corner of the aquarium near the surface of the water and among the leaves of the Nomaphila stricta. *In doing this she turned her ventral side so that the male could not get at it. This appeasement gesture puts a stop to the ritualized aggression of the male. He does not resume his driving until she returns to the open water again. At about 7 o'clock in the morning I found a totally different situation. The female no longer fled from the advances of the male, but both swam excitedly through the tank, the male frequently touching the ventral region of the female. Meanwhile they both occasionally went through picking motions in the Java moss, as if they were egg-hunting. These are however only ritualized motions, as there were no eggs released and there was no food at hand.*

Approximately a half hour later the first actual spawning took place. The male lured his mate to an appropriate spot on the bundle of Java moss. To do this he swam repeatedly back and forth between the selected spot and the female. Usually the female bit at the male first; he swam around her and made gentle beating motions in her direction. Then she finally followed to the chosen spawning site. Both stopped in the plants and suddenly the male swam to the female's side and pressed her under the leaves with his body and the male folded his caudal base over that of the female. There was a brief quivering as eggs and sperm were released, followed by the male beating away from the female and then swimming away. The female followed after a few seconds and two or three contacts later there was a pause for rest.

These observations are not the same as those of Dr. Geisler, whose Chilodus *spawned at the water's surface. He wrote: "All matings took place below the water's surface, either in the vicinity of the roots of floating plants or right in the open water. The spawning itself was so vigorous that the fish at times beat their tails out of the water and the cover glass was dripping with their splashing." Unfortunately Dr. Geisler's work does not mention if his observations were made with one or more pairs. I believe however that it was always with one and the same pair that this totally atypical behavior took place. Both of my pairs always spawned in the moss bundle at the bottom, notwithstanding the fact that the* Nomaphila *reached to the surface. The spawnings were always peaceful and without any splashing with the tails. It is hardly possible that the male in this case laid his caudal base over that of the female. My fish always mated in a horizontal position and not, as Dr. Geisler writes, "in their*

The following black and white series of photos comes from Hanns Joachim Frank. This photo shows the courting pair.

The female, in an evasive action, moves away from the male.
The male is driving the female and nipping her in the vent area.

The female now follows the male to the spawning site.

The female investigates the spawning site and picks at something at the bottom while the excited male is quivering in anxiety nearby.

The male attempts to force the female into the plants to spawn with her.

Eggs are being released as the male wraps his tail around the female in a manner similar to *arulius* on pages 76 and 77.

As soon as the eggs are released the males springs away.

Chilodus punctatus eggs immediately before hatching. The shell has just ruptured on the fish in the upper left part of the photo.

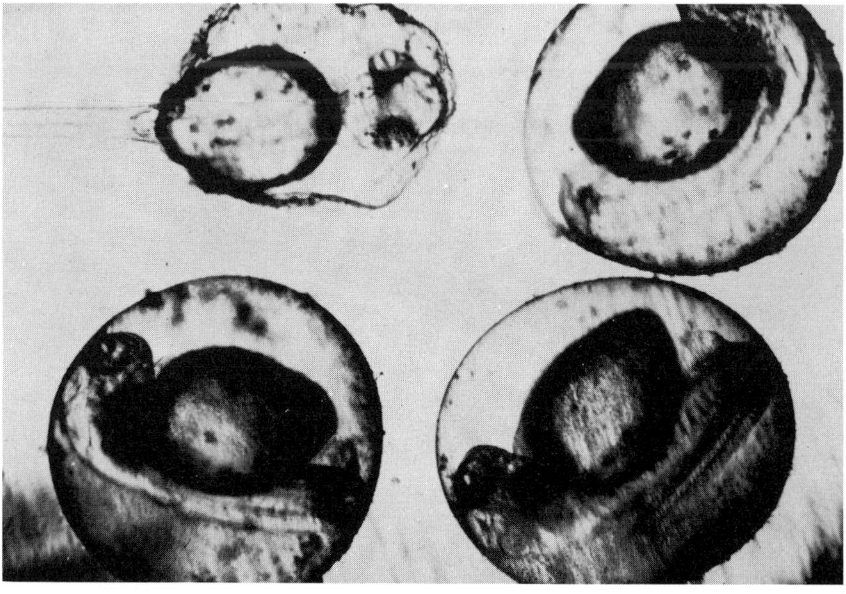

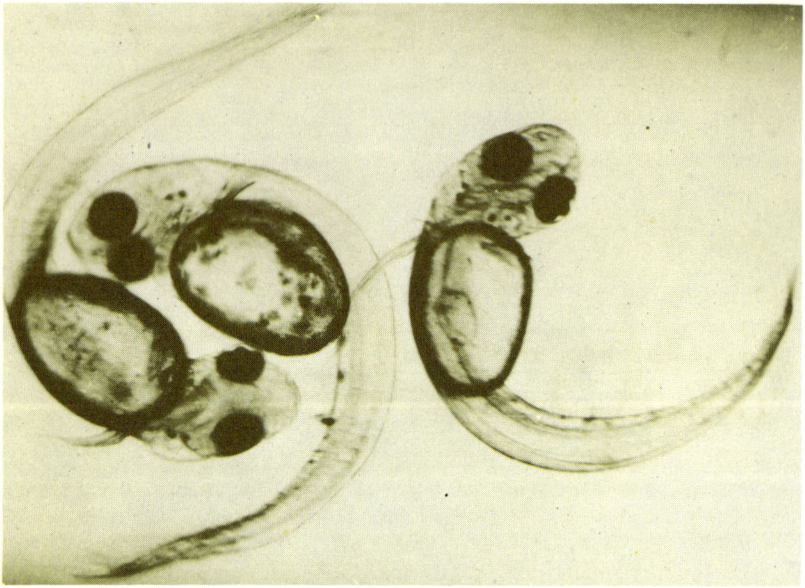

If the eggs take too long to rupture, the fry have a hardening of the spine which keeps them bent until they die a short while later.

Hannsjoachim Frank invented the technique of trying to rupture the eggs case with needles using the Chamber's micro-operative technique. Here we see a needle being inserted into the egg.

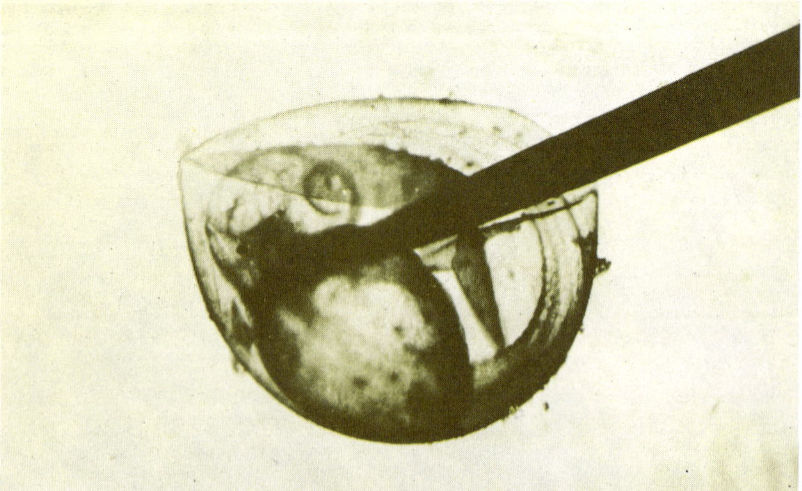

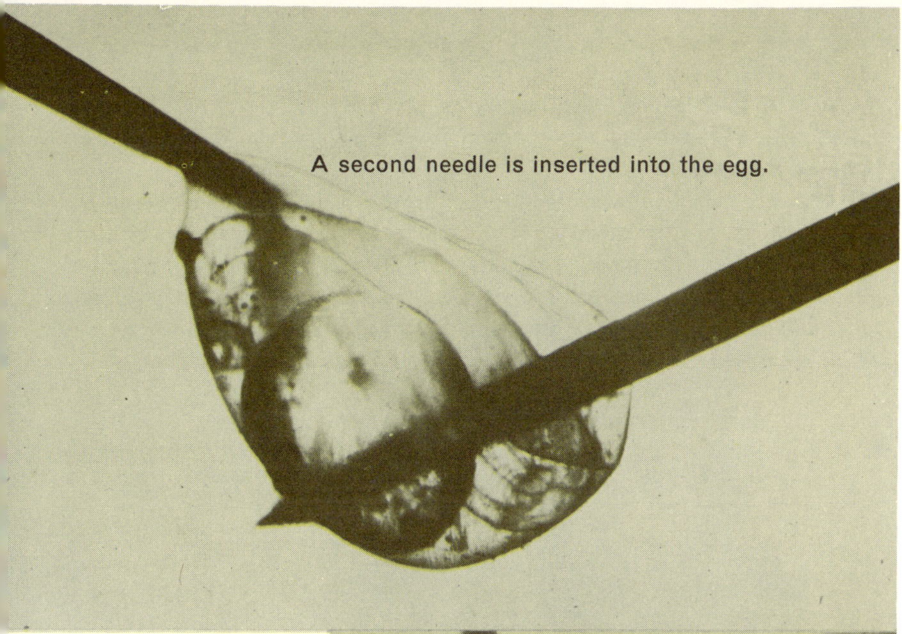

A second needle is inserted into the egg.

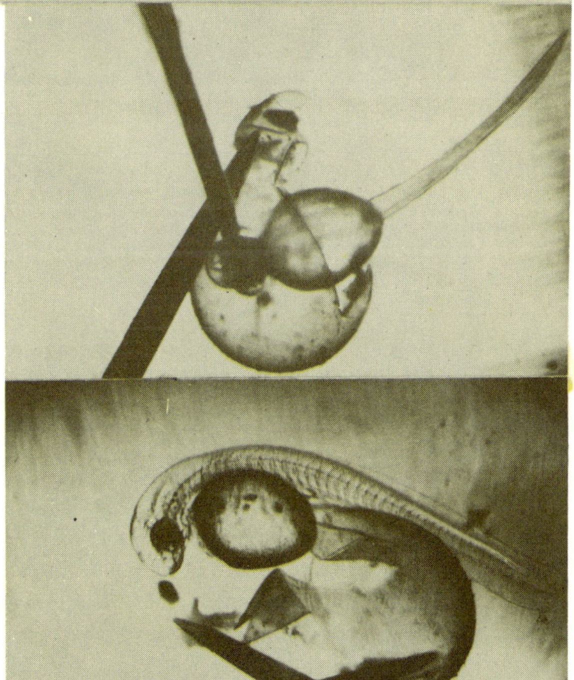

As the shell is torn with the two needles, the tail of the embryo pops out.

typically tilted position of about 60 degrees." My observations also agree with those of Brorsson, who reports on the first spawnings by Linden, in Sweden. Here also the mating act was very calm. Unfortunately many details are not mentioned.

After my spawning female had rested in the protection of the corner of the aquarium, she reacted again to the coaxing of her mate and further matings followed until her egg supply was exhausted. The black shoulder-spot vanished again and the dark horizontal line once more became visible. At this time it is advisable to remove the parents, but I could never observe that any eggs were eaten. Average output for a fully grown female is 300 to 400 eggs.

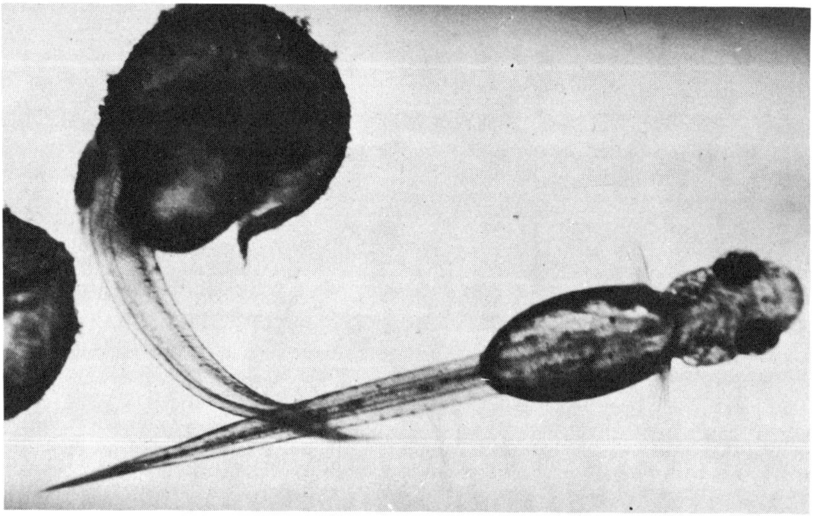

The lower egg hatched in 60 hours and the embryo is fine; the upper egg hatched in 75 hours and the fry has a crooked spine.

I prepared a table of the most important data from my observations of nine Chilodus *spawnings. From this chart I could see that the* Chilodus *spawned in rhythms which lasted from 14 to 30 days. It is interesting to note that the fish—with one exception—always spawned at an even or falling barometric pressure. On the other hand, they spawned equally well in sunny and overcast weather. Spawning temperatures were kept at 80 to 82°.*

For later spawnings, the extremely hard Gera tap water (20 to 40 DH varying by season) was used, and the fish spawned just as willingly. The fry developed normally and the egg coverings seemed to have an enormous resistance to the great calcium hardness of the water. Unfortunately I can make no exact statements as to the natural development of the eggs, because even though I raised about 1000 Chilodus *fry, only a very few hatched normally and unassisted, while the rest died fully developed. It is my guess that the egg-coverings are so hardened or acidified by a still unknown factor in the breeding water that the fry cannot break through. The eggs at the moment of ripeness were about 1.5 mm in diameter, but swelled considerably in a very short time through the absorption of water and then measured about 2.5 mm. Dr. Geisler refers to this, also the lack of adhesiveness of the eggs. Because of this they sink through the plants to the bottom. It is interesting to note the light-reflecting quality of the eggs, which causes them to shimmer in all colors of the rainbow.*

Probably the fry hatch after $2\frac{1}{2}$ to 3 days under normal conditions at about 80°. If they were freed after this time, the spinal fluid was already so hardened that they could no longer stretch themselves. They spun for a few days on the bottom and then died. I then became determined to cause the fry to hatch by artificial means, a measure which required a great deal of finesse and patience. The egg coverings seem very elastic when opened and can be stretched quite a way before they tear.

As there was no dissecting microscope at my disposal, a tool which would have made my work considerably easier, I had to work under an ordinary microscope with 20-power magnification. This made for difficult going, because the microscope gave me a reversed image. If the egg was approached with a needle from the left, the image showed the needle from the right and reversed.

In spite of this I soon became accustomed to the proper technique and was able to open the later spawnings almost without losses. The procedure goes like this: the egg is placed on a slide with a depression along with a little bit of water. Then one attempts with a fine needle to pierce through the open part of the egg center, being very careful to avoid injuring the embryo which is curled around. Then comes the most delicate job, inserting a second needle in the same hole. This done, one pulls the second needle slowly outward, often causing the egg-covering to stretch. Then it tears and usually the caudal base of the young fish is the first to free itself. Finally the egg is shaken carefully back and forth with the first needle until the embryo falls free. The tiny fish stretches immediately if the egg has been opened at the proper time.

When the eggs are opened after $2\frac{1}{2}$ days at 80°, the eyes of the embryos are still very much undeveloped. The fry hang on the glass sides or lie on the bottom until the yolk sac is absorbed and then begin to swim. According to Dr. Geisler, the young Chilodus *are free-swimming at once after hatching in 4 days at 77°. Linden's observations are more in line with mine; he says that the fry when hatched require about a week before they are free-swimming. In spite of the fact that with Dr. Geisler at most half of the eggs hatched when they got water which was treated with acriflavin and changed several times daily, there were also some deaths of fully-developed fry in the eggs. Dr.*

Chilodus punctatus

Geisler attributes this to damage of the egg coverings when they were picked up with a pipette, but I am more inclined to believe that here also the fry could not penetrate the shells and therefore died.

The young Chilodus *swim even more vertically in their first days of life than the grown-up specimens. Dr. Geisler gives a 60° angle for adult fish, and 130° for youngsters. He mentions that the youngsters "tip over," which I can do no more than confirm. Often they lie belly-up on the bottom. They are also fond of seeking shelter at the heater, on stones, or in the aquarium corners. In their first days they are almost completely transparent, and their scales are not visible until they are $\frac{3}{4}$ of an inch long.*

The newly hatched fry are immediately headstanding.

Three fry less than one inch long (actually 2 cm.).

A pair of *Nanochromis nudiceps* displaying before each other with spread fins. Photo by Ruda Zukal.

The Congo Cichlid

Nanochromis nudiceps (ansorgii)

The spelling of *Nanochromis* has recently been changed from *Nannochromis*, and some specialists feel that *nudiceps* and *ansorgii* are synonyms. The purpose of this breeding book is not to present nomenclatural arguments, but to state known facts about breeding. Unfortunately I was never successful in observing this fish breed. I always used 30 or 40 fish in a huge vat filled with 25 flowerpots and the extent of my observation was a daily inspection of the flowerpots to remove those which contained eggs. I hatched and raised the young without their parents since profit was my motive at that time. I feel this is a difficult fish to breed; not everyone agrees with me and I am going to present reports by two of the best fish photographer-breeders, and I'll let the reader judge for himself. Ruda Zukal lives in Czechoslovakia and runs the State's most beautiful tropical fish shop in Brno; Hans Joachim Richter lives in Leipzig, East Germany and fish are his hobby. The following report is by Ruda Zukal:

Soon the male leads the female to his cave which is always in a very dark, secluded corner. Photo by Ruda Zukal.

Although other observers have reported exactly the opposite, I consider Nanochromis nudiceps *among those cichlids that are not easily bred. They are peaceful toward other species of fishes as a rule, but they are not pacifists among themselves. Many fights (not only between males but also involving females) end in lethal woundings.*

This Congo cichlid reaches a length of about three inches. The body is elongated and slightly compressed laterally. The head is blunt and the forehead steep. The basic yellow coloring merges into light blue on the flanks; the belly is emerald green, and the jaws have a brassy shine. Below the eye is a shiny light-blue area; above the eye, a rusty red dash. Dark blotches along the base of the dorsal fin stand out occasionally. This fin is brownish-orange, with a white stripe beneath the black tip. The tail is yellowish with brown and orange longitudinal stripes; the upper edge is white, the lower one purple. The anal fin is purple to bright green; the ventrals are infused with green, but leading edges are white.

Sexual differentiation is obvious among adult specimens. The male is slightly smaller and a good deal less pot-bellied than the female. Coloration is similar, but the female is of a more intense emerald green, and her ovipositor is normally somewhat extruded . . . even when she is not spawning.

A pair of *N. nudiceps* with their fry swimming about their coconut shell spawning site. Photo by Hans Joachim Richter.

Nanochromis nudiceps *demands a minimum water temperature of 72° and for breeding it is recommended that as high as 79° be maintained. A tank of medium size will serve, but the water must not be hard and must always be slightly acid. In native habitat, deep caves are sought for spawning; in the aquarium, behavior is similar to that of various species of* Apistogramma *and* Pelmatochromis, *with the exception that it is the female among the Congo cichlids that takes charge of caring for the fry.*

The female, with her ovipositor still protruding, cares for her young alone. The male deserted her. Photo by Hans Joachim Richter.

N. nudiceps *is very easily startled and spends much time within its chosen retreat. Several places of refuge are best provided in the tank; if several specimens are kept together, this becomes mandatory or fierce fights will ensue. Each fish must have a particular retreat within its established territory or a state of continual war will prevail. Although not generally as belligerent as some species of cichlids,* Nanochromis nudiceps *establishes a territory and defends it against encroachment. In spawning season such action against trespassers is particularly fierce.*

The female nips the male in the region of his vent. This is shown clearly in both photos and is a definite sign of spawning progress. Photos by Ruda Zukal.

The darkest area in the aquarium will be examined for a spawning site and the eggs will be deposited in a narrow crevice between rocks if such a situation is available; if not, a flower pot with the bottom knocked out will be accepted. I had hopes of making a series of photographs of spawning activities and set

The female is now ripe, full of eggs and has her ovipositor extended to about half its maximum length. Photos by Ruda Zukal.

up slabs of slate with sharp rocks positioned on both sides to force spawning on a slanted front surface. The mated pair set to work and began excavating a pit beneath the slab. Gravel was carried away by mouth and distributed in a wide arc and before long several small piles of gravel were accumulated before the entrance to the hideout.

These preliminaries occupied both fish for several hours daily for several days. During this period courting also prevailed and the fish swam about each other with widely spread fins and from time to time the male would swim off toward the chosen spawning spot as if trying to entice the female to follow. When she did not accept his lead, both returned to the removal of gravel.

The male, in the upper photo, does everything possible to have the female enter his cave and prepare for spawning. One of his most successful tactics is to nip the female on her ovipositor. Photos by Ruda Zukal.

The female seems to enjoy having her ovipositor nipped as she doesn't flee from this attack. Photo by Ruda Zukal.

One day I noted that the behavior of the fish had changed. I lifted the slate and found a number of very small yellowish eggs. I was very much surprised to discover that there were only eleven of them as the female was two and three-quarters inches in length and had previously shown a much-distended belly and had led me to believe that a large clutch of eggs would be laid.

At this point, Mr. Zukal, having missed making a complete photographic record of the spawning and perhaps disappointed in the small number of eggs produced, terminates his report on this pair and concludes with a general observation: "The fry of this cichlid grow very slowly, and, according to my opinion and experience, it is advisable to rear the babies separate from their parents."

The male leaves his cave and the female investigates it more closely. Photo by Ruda Zukal.

The following report is by Hans Joachim Richter:

In addition to the beautiful species that make up the genus Pelmatochromis, *Africa supplies us with still another group of dwarf cichlids: the different species of* Nanochromis. *As far as recent knowledge goes, this genus includes* Nanochromis nudiceps, Nanochromis dimidiatus, *and* Nanochromis squamiceps. *All three species come from the area of the lower Congo, including the so-called "Stanley Pool," a lake-like enlargement of the lower Congo River.*

The three known species of Nanochromis *diverge a little in body shape from most fish species that come from similar habitats. It is a characteristic feature of the genus that they show an upward curve of the body; this is especially pronounced on older specimens.*

Adult male N. nudiceps *are about 2¾ inches long, while the females generally grow ¾ inch less than the males. The basic color of the elongated body is greenish-yellow. On the sides of the body and head one finds gorgeously shiny light-blue spots, while the belly of the fish glitters emerald green. Further to this we observe a delicately pink coloration above the anal fin, especially during the mating period. The dorsal fin has a white seam, which is closed off upwards by the nearly black tips of the fin rays. The upper half of the tail fin is banded in black and white, while the lower half shows a dot design.*

With a nudge and a push, above, the male gets the female to the mouth of the cave and, finally, below, she goes into the cave. This signifies acceptance of the spawning site. Photos by Ruda Zukal.

The pair begin to deepen their cave. First the male demonstrates the technique to the female and he grabs a mouthful of sand and spits it out. The female, in the photo below, quickly catches on and takes a mouthful herself. Photos by Ruda Zukal.

As soon as the male has trained the female, he merely supervises the action and the female utilizes most of her energy in doing the digging inside while the male guards the outside. Photos by Ruda Zukal.

The hole is finally dug deep enough and the pair commence spawning.
Photo by Ruda Zukal.

As far as water is concerned, N. nudiceps *is not very demanding. You may keep it in hard water as well as in soft water, but, of course, if kept in water that is soft it will show prettier colors. Water filtered through peat moss suits the fish especially well. If you want to keep* N. nudiceps *in a community tank, do so, but in this case do not forget to provide for shelter in the form of rock structures, coconut shells or inverted flower pots. The fish like to retire into such hiding places, especially right after having been put into the tank. Fundamentally,* N. nudiceps *is quite shy, but this shyness recedes a little if one refrains from changing the set-up of the tank all the time.*

It is best at first to introduce only one pair in the tank. After the fish have taken possession of a cave, this range is defended against any trespasser, and they seldom leave it. N. nudiceps *will also spawn, if kept in large tanks stocked with relatively few fishes. Under favorable circumstances you will one day see the parents leave their cave followed by a swarm of small fry. In a community tank, though, the number of young will tend to decrease, despite the attentive and intensive defense put up by the parents. After a few days the young will range so far that the parents fish will no more be able to keep an eye on them. It is then that the fry generally are victimized by the other inhabitants of the tank. If your tank is densely planted, and you are rather fortunate, a few of the baby fish will survive and grow up. Where is the aquarist, though, who will content himself with only a few young?*

If you want to raise many young from each spawning, you have to set up a special breeding tank. I use a tank measuring 28 × 12 × 10 inches for this. The bottom covering consists of a 1¼-inch layer of gravel with a granulation of about ⅛ inch, which, by the way, is the kind of bottom cover one should use for breeding all dwarf cichlids, since it fits well into their mouths when digging and rooting. Furthermore after hatching this kind of bottom prevents the helpless fry from slipping into the interstices of the gravel.

Something that is a "must" is a cave, which in my special case was represented by an overturned flower pot. This has a hole in the upper part serving as an entrance for the fish. Besides this I usually also place a few coconut shells and a driftwood root in the tank. These things offer protection to my pets during those eventual fights which, after all, will happen in any family. A couple of pieces of petrified wood and some branches of blackroot fern complete the decoration of the tank. As to technical accessories, a fine-grained air stone, set to deliver a minimum of air, is placed inside the container.

In my breeding tanks I use a mixture of tap water with a hardness of about 18° DH and rain water with about 4° DH, at a rate of 1 : 1. To this I add peat extract until the water shows a light brown color, and, in order to lower the pH value to about 6, a bit of Zoropin (a liquid plant-growth-increaser with an acid pH value, supplied by the firm of Fritz Rose, Weimar, Germany). The tank is kept under constant strong aeration during one or two days, and then the pair of breeders is released in it. The temperature should measure about 76°F. At first you will see very little of your fish, for they retire to the nearest hiding place as soon as they can, and treat themselves to a nerve-rest-cure. This they do each for himself (or herself) in separate corners of the tank. You will see the fish only the next day providing that you have not made them nervous by your own excessive proximity. Then they will inspect the tank. During this inspection trip especially the male will approach the overturned flower pot repeatedly and look inside. After this the male generally takes up permanent residence there. He then stands in the opening, having a look-see at the neighborhood. If he sees the female passing by, he generally leaves the cave in a hurry and courts her with tremblings of the body until she corresponds by also starting to tremble and swims through the tank together with him. Then they both take up their abode in the flower pot, which they leave only rarely.

The female now grows visibly rounder in the belly region, and one notices that the fish are ready to spawn very soon. Besides this, they make comprehensive preparations which extend over several days. The first thing done is to remove all pebbles from the flower pot. For this a mouthful of pebbles is taken up, carried to the entrance and spit out there. Thus a coneshaped mound of gravel is build up in front of the opening, reaching nearly up to the admittance hole. Both mates partake of this toil. In my tank I was able to observe two things, namely, that the fish preferred the flower pot as abode over all other caves, and that they cleared out nearly all pebbles. Consequently I was always able to set up the breeding tank in a manner which would permit me to watch the fish during their preparations for spawning. The only thing I had

After the young are free swimming, the female becomes very thin. Photo by Hans Joachim Richter.

to do was to place the pot with its opening turned towards the viewing pane. This also made it possible for me to photograph the fish very well while they were busy cleaning out their home.

Shortly before spawning the female becomes completely rotund in the belly region, and one clearly recognizes the extruded ovipositor. The male, too,

The female discovers the male with another brood! Photo by Hans Joachim Richter.

shows his genital papilla, but this is narrower and shorter than the female's tube.

Now the fish start courting more frequently and cleaning the inner side of the flower pot or, to be more exact, the roof of same. It is here that, after intense chasing, the eggs are deposited by the female and fertilized by the male. The yellowish-white eggs then hang from the roof by means of threads and are actively cleaned and fanned by the female. After the act of spawning is finished, the male has no more business in the cave, and has to linger around outside the pot. Now and then the female permits him a quick glance through the admittance hole, but as a rule he is chased away.

In most cases it will take the female eight to ten days to come out of the flower pot followed by a swarm of young fry. The number of young of my pair increased from about 80 at the first spawning to about 140 on later occasions. After the female has taken the brood "for a walk" for the first time, the malə becomes spruce again and keeps repeatedly edging into the swarm. At first the female does not view his intrusion favorably, but she is simply unable to get rid of him, in spite of chasing him away as many times as she can. Since the

When the male tries to return to his mate, she attacks him viciously. Photo by Ruda Zukal.

female seems to understand that this cannot be helped, soon both parents are leading their offspring proudly through the tank. The flower pot, though, remains taboo for the male at evening time, and he has to spend the night in another shelter.

It was always a special treat for me when with nightfall the small flock were put into the flower pot. The female always went in alone at first and then stuck her head out of the opening and looked around. The fry were generally still at the bottom, at the foot of the gravel heap. Jerkily they crawled up the mound, coming slowly near the opening. If this "mountain climbing" came to a stop, the female egged the small crowd on by shaking her head. She kept her head in the opening until the last baby fish had disappeared through it. Then she, too, withdrew.

In addition to the food for the parent fish, I also poured very minute Cyclops *nauplii into the tank. The young grow very quickly and are very soon eating small* Cyclops. *After about three weeks they generally reach* $\frac{3}{4}$ *inch in size, and at the age of five weeks* $1\frac{1}{4}$ *inches.*

Each spawning included some belly-sliders, though.

All in all these interesting fish gave me great joy and pleasure, and I would not ever like to miss them from my tanks. How about trying Nanochromis nudiceps? *The species isn't seen on the aquarium market as often as it should be, but you'll run into it from time to time. When you do, pick up a pair for yourself . . . you'll enjoy them.*

A pair of *Belonesox*. The male, to the left, has the usual modified anal fin characteristic of most livebearers. Photo by Ruda Zukal.

The Pike Livebearer

Belonesox belizanus

No one considers livebearing fish to be much of a challenge to breed and my initial intentions were to limit Book II to only egglaying species, but as more and more cichlid collectors are working the back waters of Central America, more and more pike livebearers are coming onto the aquarium market and not too much is known about them.

The pike livebearer belongs to the Family Poeciliidae which are the live-bearing toothed carps. Guppies, mollies, platies, swordtails and gambusinos all belong to this same family. The pike livebearer is the first or second largest member of the family and the females grow to 9 inches in length, though in aquaria they are under six inches. Males are smaller, about three to four inches.

Many color variations exist in nature and in the aquarium. Though mainly silver and green, I have seen some females that were almost completely black, while others only had a black "tuxedo." I have also seen almost colorless males and females and the accompanying photographs show, more or less, these color variations.

As with most Poeciliidae, the male has a long gonopodium. This organ is used for fertilizing the female internally and is a modification of the anal fin. The female has a normal anal fin, fan-shaped. In order for the male to impregnate the female, he must come alongside of her, rotate his gonopodium almost 180° and insert his gonopodium into

Another pair of *Belonesox*. The male is the lower fish. Photo by Ruda Zukal.

A $2\frac{1}{2}$ inch long male *Belonesox*. Photo by Ruda Zukal.

her genital pore. Some observers say he does not actually touch the female with his gonopodium but merely comes very close and shoots his sperm packets into her genital pore. From my own observations, I have seen the male make actual contact but I have not ascertained whether or not sperm is transferred during contact or preceding it.

The real problem with breeding pike livebearers is keeping them alive. Unless the fish are constantly fed they will begin to eat each other. The best food for pike livebearers is small fish. Everyone who has any success at all with pike livebearers raises quantities of guppies, platies and mollies to feed them. They make a practice of always having more food in the aquarium than the fish can eat. An eight or nine inch female can take a full grown molly in one gulp. One large female I had ate a large female molly every day for more than a month. She thrived so well on this diet that she spawned regularly. The male, on the other hand, was less than 5 inches long and he ate full grown guppies. In between they also relished live *Daphnia* if it was large enough, mosquito larvae and just about anything else that swam.

If they do not get daily rations of food they perish. The problem with most shipments of wild fish is that they are not fed for a few days between the time they are collected and the time they arrive in the petshop. These skinny fish rarely stay alive for long. The reason they die, I believe, is that they range over an area that has long been doused with DDT to kill mosquitos. The fish get the DDT into their bodies along with the dying mosquitos and dying fishes they eat. In their bodies the DDT is stored in the fish's fat where it is relatively harmless until the fish, during a few days of starvation, utilizes its reserves, and the DDT is released

A closeup of the male approaching a female with his gonopodium (modified anal fin) beginning to rotate forward. Photo by Ruda Zukal.

As the male makes sexual contact with the female, he must have rotated his anal fin a full 180° so it points forward as shown in this photo by Milan Chvojka.

from the fat and poisons the fish. This observation is hypothetical.

I have had pike livebearers checked for DDT content in their fat and it was always present, but I did not experiment with starving them and seeing whether the DDT did, in fact, enter the vital organs of the fish, and cause death.

Under aquarium conditions, pike livebearers may be kept only with larger fishes. They get along with large cichlids. If they are kept with smaller fishes they will eat them. The problem of keeping them with larger fishes is that the larger fishes might eat the guppies instead of the pike livebearers. So, if possible, keep the pike livebearers alone, just a male and female, with a school of guppies which will steadily disappear.

As the female is fertilized almost daily by the male, she will develop about 60 eggs. These eggs go through the natural maturation process of livebearing fishes and should the eggs not be fertilized, the female will spawn them anyway. The male, if active, usually fertilizes most of the eggs, but I have never had a spawning in which 100% of the eggs were fertilized. The usual number of fry is about 50, with about 20 infertile eggs. The fish spawn monthly, at 80° F.

As soon as the fry appear they are usually eaten by the parents, so you must do everything possible to hinder the breeders from eating their fry. I use a large aquarium, about 50 gallons in capacity, with two plastic screens dividing the tank into three equal parts, lengthwise. That is, if the tank has bottom dimensions of 18 ×36 inches, I

A pair of *Belonesox*. The female is barren and so slender from not eating that it is doubtful she will ever breed again. The male, the lower of the two fish, looks healthy. Photo by Ruda Zukal.

The male *Belonesox* with a newly caught guppy in his mouth. He can eat four or five of them a day! Photo by Ruda Zukal.

make three partitions of 6 × 36 inches. This sort of division gives the fry the maximum chance of escaping from the parents. The mesh of the plastic must be about $\frac{1}{8}$ inch; large enough for the babies, which are slightly more than $\frac{1}{2}$ inch long when born, but too small for the guppies to escape being eaten.

As soon as you see babies, move them to another tank and offer them copious amounts of *Daphnia*, live brine shrimp or anything small and alive, like newly hatched *Brachydanio rerio*. The fry must constantly receive live food or they will quickly perish.

If fed well, the fry can be sexed in about seven months and they will start breeding in about nine months. Pike livebearers must constantly be sorted out according to size or they will eat their slower growing brethren.

I do not recommend this fish for anyone other than as a curiosity or for a professional breeder who wants to raise large fish in an outdoor pool. By adding a few pair of pike livebearers to the outside pool they will eat all the babies, thus eliminating overcrowding in the outside pool and enabling the stock fish to grow to a large size. Many "dirt pool" farmers in Florida have a problem raising *variatus* and mollies in that the fish breed so fast, the pools are overcrowded and the fish become stunted. The pike livebearer solves that problem . . . and the by-product is profitable!

The male preparing to complete a sex act with the female extends his gonopodium. Photo by Ruda Zukal.

As the female comes closer he rotates his gonopodium farther forward (above). Photo by Milan Chvojka. Below, the male and female as the male approaches the female from behind, the usual manner in which he prepares to fertilize her internally. Photo by Ruda Zukal.

A black female above and a normal female below. Photos by Ruda Zukal.

A pair of black-lined tetras. The more slender fish is the male. Photo by Dr. Stanislas Frank.

The Black-Lined Tetra

Hyphessobrycon scholzei

What a fine story there is to be told about this fish. According to Ernst Ahl, an old German writer about things aquatic, this fish was discovered in the Amazon Basin near Pará. Since Ahl described the fish (1937), I have fished this area intensively. So have many other aquarium fishermen, because Pará is a state in Brazil and Bélém, the largest city in that state also happens to be the airport serving most of the world from Brazil, so it was quite natural that all the fish in the area would be exploited. Yet nobody ever found this

The male, in the photo above, tries to lead the female into the plant thickets. As soon as she enters, below, spawning commences. Photos by Ruda Zukal.

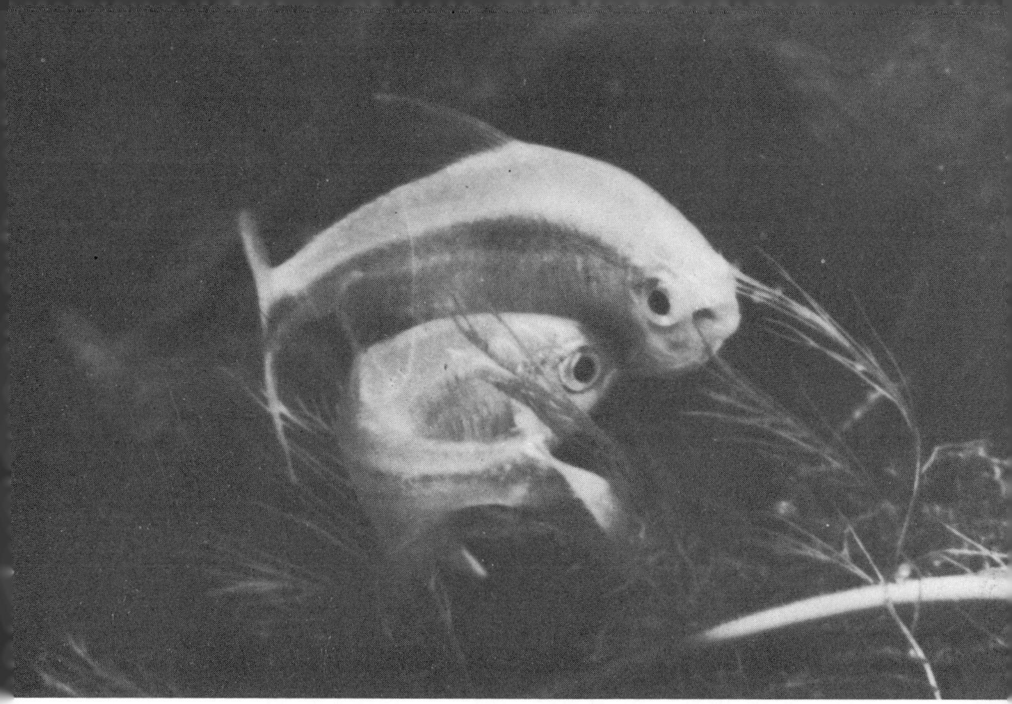

As the pair wriggle and push against each other, the eggs are extruded and as the pair separate (below) the eggs go flying all over the tank. Photos by Ruda Zukal.

A school of young black-line tetras ready for spawning. Photo by the author.

A top view of the spawning fishes. Note the eggs scattered about. Photos by Ruda Zukal.

Details of the spawning acts during which the black line tetras splash eggs in great profusion all about the tank. Photos by Ruda Zukal.

Sometimes, at the height of their frenzy, the male will wrap his body about the female. Photo by Ruda Zukal.

fish in Brazil that I know of; and I never found it either. While investigating the literature, I found that many old-timers in Germany considered this fish to be from Africa, and they called it *Aleta nigrans*. Unfortunately I didn't check this fish against *Aleta nigrans* but it is on my list of things to do!

The black-lined tetra is a very popular fish for some good reasons: it is very hardy and eats everything, it is peaceful and, mainly, it is simple to breed and the price is very low. In Florida, I merely throw out a hundred pair into a large pool measuring 25 feet wide, 150 feet long and 10 feet deep and let nature take its course. Six months later I set traps made of plastic and I trap 30,000 black-lined tetras. It's that easy.

Spawning even takes place in *Fontinalis* at the bottom of the tank. Photo by Ruda Zukal.

In the aquarium there are two ways of spawning the fish. First it is necessary to separate the sexes and feed them heavily for a few weeks. When a female is bulging with eggs, put her together with a male in a tank which has as large a capacity as possible. The minimum convenient size is about 10 gallons. Cover the bottom of the tank with spawning grass. The water should be clean, but the pH and hardness seem to be of no importance. In Florida the water is hard with a pH over 8.2 at all times. In Jersey, the water has a pH of 6.4 and is quite soft. If you have an aquarium of 50 gallons, group spawnings of the fish are practical and recommended.

Remove the fish immediately after they have spawned, which should be within 48 hours after you've put the pairs or groups together. You can induce spawning with a temperature rise of about 10° should the fish refuse to spawn the first day. The small eggs hatch in two days at 80° and the fry take another two days before they leave the glass to which they stick as soon as they are hatched. The fry are very small and must have infusoria for a few weeks until they are large enough to ingest San Francisco brand brine shrimp. Don't use Utah shrimp as they are too large and contain too much DDT.

They are an easy fish to spawn and if you are a beginner, I would suggest you start with this fish.

The Golden and Normal Ram

Microgeophagus (Apistogramma) ramirezi

There comes a time in everyone's life when he faces a tug-of-war between conscience and comfort. The honest man listens to his conscience *and gets ulcers*; the weak man takes the easy way out and forgets about the whole thing! I am one of those ichthyologists who has been emphasizing that the way a fish breeds is a definite clue to its evolution and should be considered when naming the fish and placing it in this or that genus. My colleagues said: "Axelrod, you're quite right, but we know so little about how fishes breed that science would have to hold still until technique caught up with it." I agreed and forgot about my idealistic position until a great German fish behaviorist by the name of Wickler studied the ram and said it has such a very different method of breeding, egg hatching time and spawning site, that it doesn't belong in the genus *Apistogramma* but in an entirely new genus which he proposed to be called *Microgeophagus*. Wickler is correct in that the fish doesn't breed the same way as most *Apistogramma* and it probably doesn't even belong closely related to them; but to call them "*Microgeophagus*" which means "small dirt eater" is quite beyond my imagination. He should have considered them as more closely related to *Apistogramma* and used something like *Pseudoapistogramma*. But it's too late now and whether you like it or not, the name *Microgeophagus* it is.

This fish was found a relatively short time ago, in 1947, by Manuel Vincente Ramirez in the Orinoco River system in Venezuela. It is very widespread throughout western South America and can be found wherever *Symphysodon* is not found. I have found rams in almost every river system in Colombia and Venezuela and I have read that they were also found in Bolivia (by the famed scientist Dr. Lüling of Bonn, Germany). In each habitat they have a different color and their size varies with the ecology. In small pools they grow very large and are very colorful. In shallow rivers (such as the Rio Aguaro where I found them as almost colorless gray fish), they have much less color. They grow to about three inches in length.

To say this fish is sensitive to water would be a gross understatement. I once spent several weeks in Colombia and collected some 10,000 beautiful, golden yellow rams. (Do not confuse this with the golden ram which has been developed from a mutant.) Cabling my fish farm in Florida, I had them prepare tanks, vats and outside pools for the fish. When they arrived in Florida they were split into groups and some put into each of these various containers. The tanks had soft, acid water; the vats neutral water and the pools alkaline water. Within 30 days all were dead.

The only hope for the hobby is to use those which have been bred and acclimated to aquarium conditions, but there are plenty around and my subsequent knowledge indicates that they prefer soft, acid water. Rainwater, stored for a few weeks in the dark is perfect for them. But my friend Hans Joachim Richter spawned these fish and wrote some very interesting notes about his experiences. I quote his notes as follows. By the way, compare this spawning detail with *Hemichromis bimaculatus* from *Africa.* They are Absolutely identical! EVOLUTION!

Due to the breeding behavior of this species, which diverges from that of the other Apistogrammas *(substratum; hatching time; spawning period), Wickler has established the new genus* Microgeophagus, *of which* Microgeophagus ramirezi *is the only representative.*

According to information given by the Florida importers Ramirez and Blass, the Orinoco River and Venezuela is the place of origin of the species.

New importations which, due to their divergent size, were re-classified by Mr. Meinken, of Bremen, Germany, turned out to be real M. ramirezi, *from Bolivia, from a small stream below Todos los Santos (according to authentic*

A pair of normally colored rams. The female has the bright red belly, in the photo above. Below: A golden ram male spawning with a normal female. Photos by Hans Joachim Richter.

The series of photos on this page shows the normally colored female with her very large ovipositor extended in the middle of spawning. The gold male fertilizes the eggs as the female lays them. These four photos were taken within one minute of elapsed time. Photos by Hans Joachim Richter.

data supplied by Dr. Lüling of the Ichthyological Department of the Alexander Koenig-Museum, of Bonn, Germany). These fish (males) showed a total length of 2$\frac{7}{8}$ inches and were one inch high (DATZ, 1967). The fish that were classified first showed a length of 1$\frac{3}{8}$ to 1$\frac{1}{2}$ inches, compared to 2 inches of the recently classified ones.

In Deutsche Aquarien und Terrarien Zeitschrift, *(DATZ—the German Aquarium und Terrarium Magazine) there was a polemic between Mr. Paul E. Fischer, of Caracas, Venezuela, and Mr. Meinken, based on the article of Mr. Meinken (in which he explodes another importation myth), doubting that Venezuela was the collecting site. Mr. Fischer found his* M. ramirezi *in Venezuela, however, in the Orituca, Caballo, and Guarica rivers. Since one may take it for granted that neither of the two gentlemen would supply wrong collecting data on purpose, which undoubtedly* can *happen, the range of* M. ramirezi *must be very large.*

About commercially bred specimens unfortunately one has to state that after twenty years of being kept in tanks they have lost a lot in body size and color. Today one seldom sees specimens that reach a total length of 2⅜ inches. On the other hand it should prove no problem still to breed show specimens of these fish. Many hobbyists today have large rearing tanks and this, together with the choice of the pair of breeders, is still the basic demand for breeding large and beautiful specimens. I was astonished to see the size my one hundred fry reached in a 30 gallon rearing tank in which the feeding was abundant, of course, and half of the water was changed every second day. Some of the males had turned into really gorgeous specimens with a total length of 2½ inches.

M. ramirezi *should not be considered a difficult or problem fish today, for it is a well-known fact that the species needs clear water with few chemical impurities. The initially quite ponderous question of the water hardness should be no problem any more, for today the species is being kept and bred with success in waters assaying at 40°dH and more.*

The best manner of keeping this species, which is valid for the other dwarf cichlids too, is in separate tanks for each species. The most advisable size for such tanks is 20×12×10 inches. A dark background, inside or outside the tank, helps the fish to show their real mettle. A few tree roots with some blackroot fern or java moss enhance the ornamental value of the tank. Plants should be used sparingly, dark green ones being the most advisable. A smooth dark rock (I use slabs of petrified wood which I smooth down with emery cloth) is the best spawning site for M. ramirezi. *In order to enrich the water with oxygen as well as to circulate it, either use an air stone, or else an efficient filter which also removes floating particles. Water is simply taken from the tap, with eventual acidification. This may also be done by filtration over peat moss, provided the hardness of the water is not too high. As for all fishes, the temperature may safely fluctuate a little, both from day to night and from summer to winter. This is closest to what happens in nature. As an average the species should be kept at about 77° F., and the temperature should only be raised for spawning. If you want to spawn your rams, a temperature of about 82° F. has proved favorable.*

Let us have a closer look at the species, so that we may recognize its sexual differences. The females generally are about ⅜ of an inch shorter than the males. During the spawning period the female shows a red belly region, while the males generally sport a yellowish coloration. The black shoulder spot of the male looks nearly like a cross band, while the female presents a rectangular spot which never descends below the center of the body. The shape of the head, too, permits us to recognize a difference, for the head of the male looks blunter, with that of the female giving an impression of pointedness. On the males the second and third rays of the dorsal are strongly extended, while on females this happens with the second ray only.

Choose a pair by paying attention to these characteristics, and place them in a previously prepared tank which preferably should have been set up a few days before. By the way, if you are a snail fancier, keep the spawning tank free of your pets, for they attack the spawn.

Within a few days after the fish have gotten acquainted with their new surroundings and have become familiar with the situation, the most beautiful colors show. If by any chance sunlight should strike the tank, the colors of Mr. Ram will surpass anything known so far.

Feeding the fish well, and with a water temperature around 82° F., we soon notice that the belly region of the female is a little swollen and takes on a bright red hue. This is the sign that the fish are willing to spawn. You will now soon see the first pits dug in the gravel, and you will also notice how the pair carefully clean the rock on which they intend to place their spawn. In most cases the two fish start spawning in the evening one or two days later. The female, whose ovipositor is visible now, glides a few times over the spick-and-span cleaned rock as an experiment. Then suddenly you see the first eggs stuck to the rock in a neat row. The eggs are of a yellowish-white color.

The male spends most of the time beside the rock, having a good look at everything. When the female moves a little to the side he glides over the already extruded eggs and releases his sperm, so that the eggs get fertilized. In this way the pair continually spawn for about an hour, until the female's supply of eggs is exhausted.

Caring for the spawn is performed by both parents, but the female is the more active one. The eggs are sucked clean repeatedly and fresh water is fanned over them with the pectoral fins. Meanwhile the male is actively endeavoring to create a "lunar landscape" on the bottom. Twisting his body, and shoving with his mouth he is digging craters and pits everywhere. On the other hand we can already observe the development of the eggs, for these grow darker in spots. After 36 to 40 hours, depending on the temperature of the water, the young are "peeled out" from their egg shells and transferred to one of the many pits. After all the fry have been assembled in this excavation, one of the parents seems to consider this pit the wrong one and starts the transfer of the young to the next one. Once in a while it may even happen that each of the parents takes the fry to a different pit. But shortly after this all the baby fish are gathered in the same shelter. In this way the young, even while still unable to swim by themselves, are being moved around constantly anyway. It is only four to five days later that we see the parents leading their young on their first trip abroad. The fry are now able to swim on their own. This wondrous sight will make the heart of any fancier skip some beats.

Now is the moment to give the small crew their first food. This may either be done with minute nauplii of Cyclops*, or else with freshly hatched brine*

Shown on this page are just a few of the many exciting views of his spawning rams captured on film by Hans Joachim Richter; his patient artistry was handsomely repaid by the brilliance and clarity of these magnificent photographs. Notice that the female shows the typical claret marking on the abdominal area; although this marking is heightened during the spawning maneuvers and immediately afterward, it is present in lesser degree on all in-condition female rams and is almost always shown more intensely by the female than the male.

This magnificent series of photographs shows the pair (a golden ram and a normally-colored fish) clearing a pit in the sand in which they will lay their eggs. As the female lays her eggs, the male fertilizes them (all facing page). Above the female with her fry swimming about her. Below, a closeup of the spawning pair. Photos by Hans Joachim Richter.

shrimp. The parents lead their offspring into the cloud of food, and after a few moments we will be able to see the distended bellies of the fry.

When the evening time comes, the young are again conveyed to a pit, where the parents carefully stand watch over them. It may also happen that a few of the fry stray from the flock, but they generally do not get far, for one of the parents is immediately near the escape artist grasping it in the mouth and taking it back to its brothers and sisters. Also when nauplii or infusoria have settled on one of the baby fish (which tries to shake them off), one of the parents is immediately present and cleaning the little fish by giving it a real chewing over. After ten days the young will already have reached a length of about $\frac{3}{8}$ of an inch. Now is the moment for removing the parents, or, better still, the fry, from the tank, for from now on the parental instinct of the progenitors diminishes radically.

With good feeding and repeated changes of water the fry may reach lengths of up to $\frac{5}{8}$ of an inch or a little more within a month's time. And after another month they will be marketable if all goes well.

Depending on the size and condition of the parents, one spawning of M. ramirezi *may yield from 150 to 450 fry.*

As my explanations show plainly, the spawning behavior of this fish diverges strongly from that of the other fishes of the genus Apistogramma. *This is the reason why Wickler has established the new genus* Microgeophagus. *This is quite understandable, and we should try to get used to calling our beautiful ram* Microgeophagus ramirezi.

The extended third and fourth dorsal rays almost always indicates a male ram. Compare the extended rays on this male and female. Photo by G. J. M. Timmerman.